STERNE'S ELIZA

SOME ACCOUNT OF HER LIFE IN INDIA

STERNE'S ELIZA

SOME ACCOUNT OF HER LIFE IN INDIA : *WITH HER* LETTERS *WRITTEN BETWEEN 1757 AND 1774*

ARNOLD WRIGHT, WILLIAM LUTLEY SCLATER

GYAN

Published by

Gyan Publishing House
5, Ansari Road
Daryaganj, New Delhi-110002
Phone: 011-47034999, 9811692060
E-mail: books@gyanbooks.com

Distribution Network
gyanbooks.com
India, USA, Canada, UK, Australia

ISBN: 978-93-7097-669-6 (PB)
First Published, 1923

2nd Impression 2025

Printed at: Gyan Press, Delhi.

STERNE'S ELIZA SOME ACCOUNT OF HER LIFE IN INDIA
Arthur ARNOLD WRIGHT, WILLIAM LUTLEY SCLATER

STERNE'S ELIZA

ELIZA, FROM YORICK

STERNE'S ELIZA

Some Account of her Life in
INDIA: *with her* LETTERS
written between 1757
and 1774

By

ARNOLD WRIGHT
and
WILLIAM LUTLEY SCLATER

1922

Introduction

ELIZA DRAPER, whose life, illustrated by her correspondence, is sketched in the subsequent pages, was born in India in 1744 and died in England in 1778 at the early age of 35. Her fame rests chiefly on her friendship with Laurence Sterne. But, remarkable as that association was in many ways, it was only a brief episode in her not long life, extending over but three months from the opening days of January 1767 to April the 3rd of the same year. The intimacy was broken by Eliza's embarkation for India, and as she did not return to England until 1774 and Sterne died in 1768 the two never met again.

Whether Eliza's friendship with Sterne exceeded the limits of Platonic affection must remain for ever doubtful, but it should be remembered in her favour that at the time of her meeting with the novelist she was only 24, while Sterne, much broken in health and prematurely aged, was even then entering upon the illness which terminated his existence. In such circumstances it is more difficult to imagine guilt than innocence, more especially when we find, as we do from Eliza's sprightly letters, that her impressionable nature was flattered by the attentions of Sterne, who was then at the height of his fame, a literary lion whose company was eagerly sought by those who occupied high social positions.

However this question of moral culpability may be decided, Eliza has a title to consideration quite apart from her intimacy with the author of *The Sentimental Journey*. Her letters—a number of which are printed in full for the first time in these pages, thanks to the courtesy of the late Lord Basing, amongst whose family papers they are preserved—show her to have possessed intellectual attainments of no mean order. She wrote with fluency and charm, and had a gift of graphic description which gives vitality to the scenes from Anglo-Indian life in the far-away days of the mid-eighteenth century in which she lived in Western India.

The period of Eliza's life in India coincided with the epoch-making change which converted the East India

Company from a trading venture into a great administrative body charged with the affairs of an Empire. Her first letter here published was written in the same year as Plassey was fought, and her final letter from India was penned in 1774, the memorable year in which Warren Hastings issued the proclamation announcing that the Company henceforth would directly administer the territories it had conquered. Many interesting sidelights are thrown in Eliza's correspondence on the important events which marked the progress of British domination as, in spite of some notable vicissitudes, it extended westward beyond the limits of Bengal and Madras. We catch vivid glimpses of the critical conflict with Hyder Ali, of Mysore, in the height of his power, and we are given an insight into the causes of the "regrettable incidents" on the British side which checked our arms and postponed the day of final conquest until long after Eliza had passed from the scene. But high as is the historic value of these intensely human documents, their chief interest will probably be found by the reader to centre in the sketches of Anglo-Indian life which Eliza so deftly draws. These, with her own dramatic life story, unfolded with almost painful minuteness in her letters, constitute a record of the manners and habits of expatriated Britons in India a century and a half since, which is equal to anything that the literature of that period furnishes.

A.W.

July 1922 W.L.S.

Contents

List of Portraits

Chapter I

Eliza's Birthplace

"Territory of Anjengo, you are nothing, but you have given birth to Eliza. One day these commercial establishments founded by Europeans on the coast of Asia will exist no more. The grass will cover them, or the avenged Indian will have built over their ruins; but if my writings have any duration the name of Anjengo will remain in the mind of man. Those who shall read my works, those whom the winds shall waft to thy shores, will say: 'It is there that Eliza was born'; and if there is a Briton among them, he will hasten to add with pride: 'and she was born of English parents.'"—Abbé Raynal's *Histoire philosophique et politique des établissements et du commerce des Européens dans les deux Indes.*

Far down the Malabar Coast, seventy-two miles from Cape Comorin, the southernmost point of India, on a narrow spit of sandy soil, is an insignificant fishing village. A mere cluster of huts, squalid and unkempt, dotted about a misshapen mound of ruins, the settlement to-day is all that represents Anjengo. The massive walls of its once imposing fort are level with the dust; the "capital Government House and commodious square" of an earlier day have utterly vanished and an advancing tide of tropical growth has submerged the pathetic little plot of ground in which the old factors and writers of the eighteenth century, stricken with the rigours of a deadly climate, found their last resting place. In its desolation Anjengo suggests the lines of the Persian poet Sadi:

The spider holds the veil in the palace of Cæsar;
The owl stands sentinel on the watch towers of Afrasiab.

A forlorn derelict, it speaks, however, not of the retributive justice of the Abbé Raynal's rhapsody but of the vicissitudes of a commerce influenced by purely utilitarian tendencies and flowing in the channels best suited to it. In days far remote when pepper was a commodity of supreme importance in the transactions of the East India Company, Anjengo, as the natural outlet of a rich agricultural territory in Southern India, had its uses ; but when the time came, as it did towards the end of the eighteenth century, when the erstwhile traders became conquerors and administrators, this purely commercial factory was no longer worth the cost of its maintenance and it fell into neglect and obscurity. Its fate differed in no degree from that of other early centres of the trading period in India. Who to-day, for example, can say where Fort David was situated ? Who can state in what region the settlement of Natal (not the South African State) was planted, or define the precise location of Fort Victoria ? Relics of a dead past, they have faded almost completely out of remembrance. And Anjengo ? You will look for it in vain on many modern maps of India. The trader passes it contemptuously by as beneath his notice, and the hordes of tourists who continually stream through Colombo, less than a day's sail yonder to the south, are completely ignorant of its existence, though they will undergo fatigue and risk fever in tracing the outlines of the " dead cities " of Ceylon, and spare no effort to get a glimpse of the bit of ivory which a convenient tradition identifies with one of the teeth of Buddha. From year's end to year's end, in fact, an English foot is seldom planted on the soil of Anjengo, and rarely a thought is given to its memories.

And yet we ought not to need the Abbé Raynal's

fervid apostrophe to remind us that this slip of Malabar sand is classic ground to the British people. Here for a century or more the national flag was kept flying—a mark for East Indiamen, many of which at this spot made their first landfall on arrival off the Indian coast ; here a prosperous trade was for generations carried on with regions to which the Romans resorted for the spices and the various odorous products which were essential to their luxurious mode of life ; here, coming to the purely human interest, was the birthplace of Robert Orme, the talented author of the famed *Historical Fragments*—the Thucydides of Anglo-Indian history ; and here, lastly and most important of all for our purposes, first saw the light of day Elizabeth Sclater, or, as she is better known, Eliza Draper, she who to Sterne was more than Stella was to Swift, Maintenon to Scarron, and Sacharissa to Waller—the Eliza who inspired the Abbé Raynal to pen what all in all is the greatest tribute ever paid by a Frenchman to an Englishwoman's genius.

Anjengo at the time when our narrative commences had been close upon half a century in British occupation. It came into the possession of the East India Company in 1694 through a grant from Queen Ashure of Attinga, a principality largely identified with the modern State of Travancore. This sovereign was one of a line of royal females who ruled by a peculiar tenure somewhat analogous to that of the Mahratta Princes of Poona. The real power was in the hands of Brahmins, and the queen was only allowed to have a voice in court concerns and matters of no great significance. Nevertheless, as an account of the Attinga Kingdom written by an Anjengo official in 1704 informs us, all business was transacted in her name with great formality, and her subjects greatly reverenced her, always "calling her Tombrane, which is to say goddess." Reverence there may have been, but her qualities were hardly those which pertain to a deity. Abominable cruelties were practised in her name if not with her sanction. Grose tells a story, which Forbes of *Oriental Memoirs* fame, himself for a period an Anjengo official, confirms, of one of these Attinga queens who ordered the breasts of a female servant of an English lady at Anjengo to be cut off because the unfortunate woman had appeared before her attired in a bodice given her by her mistress and worn by her in opposition to the universal custom of the country, which was and is for women to go about with the upper part of their bodies unclothed. Another episode in which the savagery of this strange dynasty was revealed occurred in the early years of the eighteenth century, when nearly the whole of the Company's servants at Anjengo, including the Chief Factor, were massacred while on a visit to the queen. The entire conditions of life at this settlement were extraordinary for a period long after this disaster. Forbes in his most readable book gives a very vivid picture of what the place was like when he lived there in the year 1772.

We gather from his interesting pages a strong impression of the isolation of the little band of exiles who represented British influence in this remote corner of India.

Unfortunately the official records tell us little of the transactions of the years in which we are most concerned with Anjengo. A peculiarly voracious breed of white ants made a meal of the bulk of the old archives in some distant period ; what remains are mere fragments, mostly unimportant accounts or details of trading transactions ; still, it is possible here and there to get glimpses of this obscure little world into which the subject of this biography was born on April 5, 1744. But before we deal with these scraps of paper it is desirable to give some account of Eliza's parentage.[1] Her father was May Sclater, the son of the Reverend Christopher Sclater (1681–1737), who was the Rector of Loughton and subsequently of Chingford in Essex. He obtained his rather peculiar Christian name—a name which has been a pitfall to more than one writer —from his mother, Elizabeth (1685–1743), daughter and heiress of John May of Worting, near Basingstoke. Those were days of large families, and May was one of thirteen children. Seven of these attained maturity, and it was among them, her uncles and aunts and their children, her cousins, that Eliza spent her early life, while it was in the main with them that she carried on the correspondence which figures later in these pages.

For the sake of completeness it may be useful to go a little deeper into these family connections, a knowledge of which is desirable as a preliminary to the study of the letters.

The eldest of the uncles was Dr. William Sclater (1708–1778), who followed his father's footsteps, entering the church and succeeding his father as Rector of Loughton. In 1771 he was appointed by the Grocers' Company Rector of St. Mary-le-Bow in Cheapside, London. He was accidentally killed by a sack of carraway seeds falling on his head from a crane as he was walking up St. Mary-at-Hill in 1778.

Christopher Sclater's second surviving son was Richard (1712–1754), who was in business in London and a member of the Grocers' Company. He was an Alderman for the Farringdon Ward Within of the City

[1] *See* Descent of Eliza Draper, p. 191.

of London ; he died, however, before Eliza reached England for the first time. His first wife was Magdalen, daughter of John Limbrey, of Hoddington in Hampshire, by whom he had two children—Thomas Limbrey, afterwards Thomas Limbrey Sclater Mathew (1742–1809), and Elizabeth (1744–1814). Eliza was devoted to these two cousins and saw a good deal of them both when she was in England as a child and subsequently when she brought her children home in 1765, and much of her correspondence was with them, especially with Thomas. She appears to have had for him a more than cousinly affection. "All my kinsfolk," she writes later, "are, in comparison of thee, as trifling as my little finger to my two bright eyes."

Neither Thomas nor Elizabeth ever married, and both of them in turn succeeded to Hoddington after the death of their uncle John Limbrey in 1802, but this, of course, was long after Eliza's death.

Richard Sclater's second wife was Penelope, daughter of Philip Lutley, of Bromecroft Castle and Lawton, in Shropshire. By this second marriage there were two children—Bartholomew Lutley (1753–1804) and Penelope Lutley (1752–1843). After Richard Sclater's death in 1754 his widow lived in her own house at Worcester, where she was visited by her niece Eliza.

Another uncle of Eliza was Joseph Sclater (1715–1769). He was in business in London and succeeded or was a partner of his brother Richard as a druggist in Newgate Street. He is alluded to in one of Eliza's letters in rather a contemptuous manner as "drugs."

After this somewhat long digression we may return to May Sclater, whom we have left earlier on the threshold of his Indian career. Entering the Company's service in August 1736, at the age of 17, Eliza's father spent fourteen months at the India House in acquiring the rudiments of a cadet's training, and was then sent out to Bombay as a writer on the princely salary of £5 per annum. He appears to have made good progress in his work. At all events, as early as 1738 he figures in the records as Assistant Secretary at Bombay Castle, and on December 4, 1741, is revealed as Secretary of Anjengo, with, as his chief, Charles Whitehill, who subsequently became his father-in-law. Whitehill was a man who had spent a long life in the country when May Sclater first made his acquaintance. He arrived in India before 1715, as he is mentioned in a list of the civil officials in Bombay in that year, together with his wife Sarah and his son John. Of Judith Whitehill, Eliza's mother, we know little beyond that she is included in a list of the European inhabitants of Bombay now at the India Office, as an unmarried woman in 1740–1, and as a widow with a daughter Mary in 1746–8. Judith's mother is a much more tangible person. There is a story in the Blakeway MS.[1] (now in the Bodleian) that Mrs. Whitehill was captured by the notorious western India pirate Angria and held to ransom until a substantial amount had been paid by the husband. There is no confirmation of the statement in the official records of the time, but it is likely enough that the episode actually occurred, as it was a favourite device of Angria to levy blackmail in this fashion on the leading members of the European community.

Mrs. Whitehill appears to have predeceased her husband. It is possible that she was alive at the time of the marriage of her daughter to May Sclater, but

[1] Vol. iii, p. 304.

there is no subsequent mention of her either in the official lists of Europeans at the Company's settlements or in the correspondence which will be introduced later.

Charles Whitehill himself is a prominent figure in Western India annals of the mid-eighteenth century period. We find his name in the Factory Records of Anjengo for February 16, 1725–6, where his signature appears immediately after that of Alexander Orme, the father of the historian, who was Chief of the settlement at the time. A little later, on April 20, 1727, Whitehill's name is given as warehousekeeper on a salary of £40 per annum with a monthly allowance of 500 fanams. On January 18, 1739–40, Whitehill signs the General Letter periodically prepared for the information of the superior authorities as Chief. We also have record of the acknowledgment he made of his appointment to the superior position, an acknowledgment couched in the usual fulsome language deemed appropriate to such occasions, and containing an expression of his intention to exercise his greatest care "to continue the settlement in the same tranquility it has enjoyed of late years." Whitehill amassed considerable wealth in the Company's service. He was probably a rich man at the time of May Sclater's marriage to his daughter. He owned either then or subsequently valuable house property in Bombay, and a part of this, in the heart of the fort, he disposed of in 1767 to the Company for the large sum of R40,000. To complete his history it may be stated that he retired from the service about the middle of the century, was living at Worfield in Shropshire in 1751, and died there at an advanced age in 1788, leaving the bulk of his property to his second wife for her life, with legacies to the children of his son Stephen, " now in service of the East India Co., Bombay," and devising the residue of his estate to his sons John and Stephen. There was a third son, Thomas, who died earlier after a long career in India. John Whitehill, the second son, played an important part in the drama of Eliza's life, as the narrative will disclose. He was also conspicuous as a leading participator in some of the curious political transactions which stirred the life of Madras and eastern India in the second half of the eighteenth century. A fuller reference to his personality and career may be left to the later chapters to which the story of his official life properly belongs.

No record exists of May Sclater's marriage to Judith Whitehill. Traditionally the ceremony is believed to have taken place in Bombay Cathedral. This is in accordance with probability. At the time there was only one chaplain on the Company's establishment in Western India, and it would have been rather exceptional, if not extraordinary, if the hard-worked cleric then in charge had travelled 600 miles to Anjengo, a journey involving probably several weeks' absence from the Presidency, to unite the young couple. The whole of May Sclater's wedded life is somewhat shadowy. All that is certain is that three children were born of the marriage, Eliza and two sisters, Mary and Louisa, and that both the parents died while their offspring were very young. May Sclater's death occurred probably in 1746, and that of his wife two years subsequently.

It must have been upon the grandfather that the charge of the three young orphans devolved on the demise of their parents. Charles Whitehill had a handsome house in what was then the best residential part of Bombay. It looked out across a green upon which the troops exercised, and had as a near view the gaunt outlines of the Cathedral, then standing in severe isolation to the left of the Whitehills' home. Time has completely transformed the locality. Only in some of the older buildings in the narrow streets of what is still called the Fort, though the walls have long since disappeared and scarcely a vestige of the old military character of the area remains, will you have a reminder of the period a century and a half since when Eliza and her sisters under the charge of some kindly dark-skinned servitor took their airing upon the green and possibly wandered out beyond the walls to the open expanse which stretched away to the shores of Back Bay. A subdued, melancholy existence must have been theirs with few English children of their own age to keep them company and nothing to relieve the dull routine of life in a tropical climate. Facilities for education were practically non-existent in this early Bombay. Some years earlier than the period of May Sclater's death the Bombay Council had written home intimating that they had "often endeavoured to appoint a schoolmaster to instruct the youth of the settlement, but without success for want of a person qualified," and they had implored the directors to send some efficient teacher from home. But it is doubtful whether anything was done beyond making provision for the education of the children of the soldiers and subordinate officials.

In the higher official circles the practice prevailed of sending children to England as soon as they were old enough to leave their parents. Following this custom, Eliza and her sisters were despatched home to receive their schooling. Eliza seems to have been about ten years of age when she thus made her first acquaintance with the homeland. Apparently the girls were entrusted to the charge of their aunt Elizabeth (1714–1769), the wife of the Reverend Thomas Pickering, Vicar of St. Sepulchre's, the famous church hard by Newgate whose bell tolled the knell of generations of condemned prisoners up to the end of the period in which that grim London prison was the scene of executions. As the correspondence to be given later will reveal, the most affectionate ties were formed between the good vicar and his wife and their young charges, and they could hardly have fallen into better hands. St. Sepulchre's Vicarage, however, was only the occasional home of the children. They were entered at some boarding-school for young ladies, one of many such which existed on the outer fringe of London in that period.

In after days, in a letter addressed from India to her friend Mrs. James, in England, Eliza gave, in the form of advice about the choice of a school for a young girl, a sketch of boarding-school life which must have been largely the fund of her own experiences.

I DETEST boarding schools [she wrote], I know from having experienced it in my own case, how little of the useful is to be acquired there and I am truly sensible of the risque a child runs of being ruined in her constitution and for ever corrupted in her morals in those seminaries—for in order to secure both the one and the other—every child it associates with ought to be of as amiable propensities as itself—and can this be expected where there are fifty children, all descended from different parents—no one of which may be like the other, in either affections, humor or blood. And who of feeling can be satisfied to trust the chance for that which is to contribute the honour and welfare or disgrace and misery of a beloved child? For 'tis certain that the principles inculcated in youth, and confirmed by habit, more or less influence all our succeeding actions and creates the portion of praise, or blame, which fixes our character in life. I have thought often and very much on this matter and the more I ponder it, the more I am confirmed in my just partiality for a home education.

In another part of the same letter Eliza laments the defects in the education of girls of good parentage of her day.

As my reflection increases [she observed], I daily am more sensible of the loss I have sustained in not receiving those advantages which are the birthright of girls well born or by nature sociable, especially if their prospects are such as to give them a chance of being fixed in conspicuous life—such was my case—it is the case of all girls destined for India—No beings in the world are less indebted to education—None living require greater assistance from it—for the regulation of time in Eastern countries is such that every woman must naturally have a large portion of it; Leisure—this is either a blessing or a curse as our minds are disposed. The majority of us are extremely frivolous; this I grant. How should it be otherwise? We were never instructed in the importance of anything but one world point, that of getting an establishment of the luxurious kind, as soon as possible. A tolerable complexion, an easy manner, some degree of taste in the adjustment of our ornaments, some little skill in dancing a minuet and singing an air are the *summum bonum* of perfections here (India)—and these are all that mothers, aunts and governesses inculcate with some merit into the accomplishments—the very best of us—leave Europe and commence (as) wives in the East at fourteen. Climate, custom, and immediate examples induce to indolence—this betrays us into the practise of gallantry—that poisoner of all that's amiable and good.

The whole tenour of Eliza's allusions to education in her letters indicates that her school life was not happy. Especially significant is the stress she lays throughout upon the vacuity and frivolity of the conventional young lady's training of the period. She referred on one occasion to the demoralisation of "Parlour Boarder Maxims" and their influence in promoting proficiency "in all those flirtations and flippancies so commonly found in Women Girls." Manifestly, there was much in Eliza's school training to which in her maturer years she did not look back with favour. It would almost seem that it was to those early deficiencies that she attributed the shipwreck of her happiness by a premature and ill-assorted marriage. But we must not speculate. Eliza's school training is over, and the good ship Anson is waiting to take her and her sisters to India to enter upon the career which fate has assigned to each of them. In May 1757 they embark on the voyage which seven months later is to restore them to their grandfather's home in Bombay.

Chapter II

ELIZA *returns to* INDIA *and* MARRIES

In point of years Eliza was a veritable child when she returned to Bombay in 1757, but in experience and bearing she was a woman—a true type of that order of Women Girls of which she in after years wrote with so much strength of feeling. There is an amusing assumption of airs of maturity in her earliest letters, given in later pages. The writer might have been, not, as he was, a girl who was barely in her teens, but as woman well acquainted with life. There was no doubt a good deal of pose in the picture she painted of herself. But allowing fully for that there remains much to indicate an exceptional precocity of intelligence both in her and her sister Mary, whose earliest Indian letter also figures below. The voyage itself must have contributed to the girls' education in the ways of the world, and particularly those which have to do with the tender passion. Cooped up for more than half a year on an East Indiaman of no greater tonnage than a modern coasting brig, the very mixed body of passengers could not have failed to offer many points of close study for the inquiring minds of these eager schoolgirls, intent on taking their full share of all that life had to offer.

Eliza had been only a short time in Bombay when she penned the following letter (No. 1 of Lord Basing's collection) to her cousin Elizabeth Sclater :

I AM doing myself the pleasure of writing to my dear Cousin according to promise and will give her a faithful account of our Voyage and all the Curiositys that we came to this part of the world. We arrived safe at Bombay two days after Christmas day and was seven long months on our passage on board a ship.

I was never half so much rejoiced at going to any Ball in my life as when we first saw the land; we was five months before we ever saw anything but sky and water and you may be sure to us the sight was very agreable. We then went to a place called Galley[1] a Dutch Settlement where there could none of the people talk Inglish which was very disagreable to us. There was three Ships besides ours was at the same place which made it better than it else would have been. The Dutch people are white but their Servants are all Black, they wear nothing at all about them but a little piece of rag about their waste, which to us at first apeared very Shocking. When we went on shore at this place we was put into a pelenkene which is in the form of what I cannot tell what to describe to you. It is carryed by four men. There is a bed in it so that if you have any inclination for sleeping in it you may. I think wee met with nothing else in our passage that is worth relating; in short my dear Cousin, people talk of such Wonders as are to be seen in the Indies and yet I'll declare to you that I have not seen any one thing in particular that is worth writing you word of. Bombay is a pleasant place but nothing extraordinary fine about it. The coolest time of the year is now so that I can't tell you how I like that part of the year which is so very warm and sometimes fatal to them that have not Strong Constitutions. My Pappas house is the best in Bombay and whare a great deal of Company comes every day after dinner. They allways Instead of water glasses the Servants bring what they here call guglet and gindy almost like a wash hands bason to wash yourself after meals. There is another Custom which I am come into that of Sleeping in the afternoon and never wear Caps which we at first thought a little Strange. I forgot to tell you in the first part of my letter that on Christmas, New Years and the Kings birthday

[1] Point de Galle in Ceylon.

there is allway a publick Ball, we was as unfortunate enough to come the day after the Christmas one but saved New years, and now my Dear Cousin I think I have told you all the news that is in my power and I hope that you will not be Deficient in sending me all that you can. I'll advise what you shall do so you must in the first place make a writing paper Book and as anything pleases you set it down and by that means when you come to write me a very long letter which I do assure you I shall expect you will not be at a loss what to say to me. You cant expect so long a one from me now but next time I write you shall find that I keep my word with you. I shall do the same way myself as I told you of and then you may read my letters out to my Aunts and Uncles and let me beg of you my Dear to do so as nothing will give me greater pleasure than hearing from you and as our Correspondence cant be very frequent let me beg of you to let slip no Opportunity of Obliging me in that particular. Pray make my compliments acceptable to all your acquaintance Mr. and Mrs. Hillesdon and the young ladys, to your Brother pray give my love and tell him if he will do me the favour of writing me a line I will do myself the pleasure of answering it. Upon no other Conditions tell him from me will I even Condescend to Inquire after him or ask so much as how he does; tell him I will forget he is my Cousin and disown he is so, if he comes to India I will take no manner of notice of him but I dare say I shall have a very long and agreable letter from him and as for you I expect three large sheets of paper at least. From me you cannot expect so much because I have a great number you but one. The Ships are now on their Departure from England I hope that by them you and the rest of my Dear Friends have not forgot to write me. I shall be very impatient for their comeing and I hope I shall not be disappointed and now my dear I think I have wrote you great deal so wishing you your health and happiness I conclude myself your very afectionate

ELIZ. SCLATER.

From several points of view this lively epistle is of interest. On its personal side we get a suggestion of that deep attachment of Eliza for her cousin Thomas

Limbrey Sclater which colours all her correspondence. He was to have her love, and she wished him to know that she would appreciate a letter from him. To such she would reply, but if he should dare to be remiss in this respect she would disown him. This was the first of many playful passages in which Eliza indulged in raillery at the expense of her cousin. As will be seen as the narrative proceeds, not the least charming element of the correspondence is the revelation it makes of a boy and girl fancy, deep and enduring on Eliza's side at least, but never destined to reach fruition.

In its illumination of Bombay social customs in the mid-eighteenth century period Eliza's letter is of importance. We are given here quite a vivid picture of the home life of a leading British resident of the time. We see the family sitting down at midday to what doubtless is a heavy dinner, and we note that at the meal's close there is a circulation of "the guglet and gindy"—a sort of "wash hands bason." Then there was the afternoon sleep followed by tea, at which, for the first time in the day, the ladies donned their finery. They wore no caps, however, greatly to Eliza's surprise, but if Grose, who visited Bombay in this period, is correct they made up for the omission by a plentiful display of patches. According to an amusing story he tells, one lady with her face extensively adorned in this fashion who was visiting with her husband a local prince excited on account of her spotty complexion the sympathy of the exalted host, who expressed to the husband on leaving his fervent hope that the lady would soon be rid of her boils! To return to Eliza's "Pappa's" household, we find that it was the custom of the time for friends to drop in in an unconventional way at the close of the day for gossip and possibly music and cards. It was all very friendly and intimate, and suggests, what was indeed the case, that the English community of the settlement was so small as to partake of a family character.

It was probably at one of these evening assemblies in the commodious old house in the Fort that Eliza met her fate in the person of her future husband, Daniel Draper. It must have been on his side at least a case almost of love at first sight, for within four months of Eliza's landing in Bombay the marriage took place, the actual date of the ceremony being July 1758. At the time Eliza was a little over fourteen years of age, while her husband was thirty-four. The disparity of age was not the least drawback to the union. In temperament the pair were quite unsuited to one another. While Eliza was of a lively disposition, full of the joy of life, Draper was morose and reserved, the victim of "nerves," and suffering from a spasmodic complaint of the right arm—a sort of writer's cramp brought on by overmuch industry with the pen in his official capacity. He was a poor sort of creature altogether to mate with a vivacious, impressionable girl of the character of Eliza. Neither temperamentally nor intellectually had they anything in common. In such a union sooner or later there was bound to be disagreement, more or less serious as the conditions of their married life brought into play the antagonistic elements latent in the couple.

The Drapers, like the Whitehills, were a well-known family in India at the time of Eliza's marriage. Early in the century there were three permanent officials of the name in the Company's service—Joshua, who went out to Madras in 1715 and became a Member of Council in that Presidency; Ingleby, the father of the famous General Sir William Draper, who served in

Bombay ; and William Henry Draper, who also served in Bombay. The three were probably brothers, or at all events nearly related. William Henry Draper was the father of Daniel Draper. He was a man of considerable prominence in the Company's service in Western India—a typical specimen of the free living, money-seeking official of his day. We have some not altogether edifying sidelights thrown on his character in the records. He appears in an entry of the Bombay Council's General Letter of the date of January 1, 1727–8, as the fighter of a duel at Gombroon (the modern Bunder Abbas), where he was Chief at the time. In the " very disagreeable account " which had reached them of this fracas the Council were informed that the facts were as follows : " Mr. Draper challenges and fights Mr. John Fotheringham, and after they were parted William Cordeux joins with him to dispossess Mr. Draper, but were prevented by the soldiers adhering to their duty." Mr. Draper, it was added, had suspended both his antagonists, but the Council had thought it advisable on their part to suspend Mr. Draper himself. William Cordeux, who was a "loose, vicious person," was detained in Bombay to be sent home by the first available ship.

William Draper's prospects do not appear to have been greatly prejudiced by the Gombroon episode. In 1726, when a Charter was granted by the King creating a Mayor's Court at Bombay, Draper was appointed the first Mayor under the new constitution on a yearly salary of R500. In the same year his wife, Theodosia, died. She is described in the legal documents appointing Draper as executor of her estate (she died intestate) as " relict, before her marriage with you William Henry Draper, of Robert Sutton, and executrix of the will of her first husband Stephen Strutt." Some time later, about the year 1737, Draper figured considerably to his disadvantage in the will of a certain Elizabeth Vachery, "widow and relict of Captain Joseph, late of Bombay." After bequeathing to her slave girl Clara "all her joys[1] and wearing apparel" and also "her freedom and liberty," she devised the residue of her estate to "Mr. Charles Whitehill, Chief of Mahim, and Captain Samuel Walker, of Bombay, for the benefit of her dear adopted son Philip Pilgrim, a child given to my late husband by Wm. Henry Draper, of Bombay, Esquire." The testator desired that the executors should see the child educated and brought up as they should think proper, and on his arriving at fit age "put him out as apprentice," but (the will proceeded) in case it should happen that the mother of Philip Pilgrim or Mr. Draper his reputed father should at any time or times give them any trouble or molestation about his education or bringing up "then the legacy was to be null and void." What ultimately happened to this interesting charge we do not know. Nor is there much further light thrown on William Draper's career in the records.

William's son Daniel Draper, Eliza's husband, was born in 1726, and, therefore, must have been the offspring of a second marriage of the elder Draper; he was probably sent to England when quite young to be educated. His name appears, together with those of his sisters Anne and Theodosia Draper and his brother Cowan H. Draper, in the lists for 1728–9 and 1729–30, and after that it is not again recorded until 1749, when he arrived in Bombay as a writer in the Company's

[1] Jewels, from the Portuguese *joia*. A word in common Indian use to the eighteenth century.

Bombay establishment. His first appointment was to the office of Marine Paymaster, a post which must have brought him into close association with Commodore James, in whose family circle Eliza first met Sterne. Whatever may have been Daniel Draper's failings as a husband, he proved himself to be an assiduous and efficient official. Such was his zeal that at the age of twenty he was appointed Secretary and Portuguese Secretary to the Government. Subsequently he was entrusted with a rather important mission to Jedda in the Red Sea, and later still he is revealed as holding the responsible position of warehousekeeper at Gombroon. When he met and married Eliza he was well on the high road to lucrative office and, therefore, in a worldly sense, was a thoroughly eligible husband.

Marriage came almost as a matter of course to all well-bred English girls who landed in Bombay in these remote days. It is, therefore, not surprising to find that Eliza's example was quickly followed by her sister Mary, who, on April 2, 1760, was wedded at the age of fourteen and a few months to Rawson Hart Boddam (1734–1812), a young writer who subsequently became Governor of Bombay. His career will occupy attention later, and, meanwhile, we may introduce a striking letter from the young wife addressed to her uncle, the Reverend Thomas Pickering, the Vicar of St. Sepulchre's, which is preserved in Lord Basing's collection at Hoddington.

BOMBAY, *Nov.* 18, 1760.

DEAR Doctor,—As I have an opportunity thro' my Papa proceeding to Europe to pay you my respects and to acquaint you with my change of situation having followed my sister Draper's example by comitting Matrimony with Mr. Rawson Hart Boddam and for whose character I shall refer you to my Papa, all I can say is that it was intirely agreable to the wishes of my friends in this part of the Globe, and that I am extrarny happy in the Choice I have made.

The misfortune that befell my cousin betsy's husband Mr. Vanderdujsens sea horse by running away, deprived your friends here of much real satisfaction ; it was a noble conveyance for wafting you to these distant climes, and had your scheme taken place it would have been a prodigy in Asia.

I borrowed a hint from you of a vehicle by asking a friend of my husbands one Mahomet Soffa a wealthy Merchant in these parts to send an express over land purposely to acquaint you of my having consented to change my Condition with an invitation to you my Aunt and Mr. S. and Mrs. Vanderdujsen to be at the celebration of my Nuptials at Bombay within four months from the date of writing to you, but before I gave my consent to my young man I made this proviso, that I should wait single 3 months and 15 days unless my scheme was averted by some unforeseen accident.

Mr. Mahomet Soffa undertook to send a Conveyance and promised that my packett should be as snugly and as safely conveyed as an egg in a Duck's belly ; he proposed for safety that I should send an Ostrich, with one of his carrier Bagdet pidgeons for his guide, and that the ostrich should swallow the Letters and take flight for Amsterdam to arrive by a certain limited time ; after the ceremony was offered for their success (as is customary in these eastern countries) the birds sallied forth post haste, and the Merchant assured me this was a swift carriage and that I might depend on less than twenty five days the ostrich and pidgeon would be in Holland with your friend Vanderdujsen, to whom I sent advices for forwarding the packett with the utmost dilligence to London. In my Letters I informed you that Mahomet Soffa had prepared a kickery or coach at a certain place in Germany drawn by four flying Camells which would bring you to Bombay in two months.

My letters bore date the 1st of January, I fixed my Marriage day the first of April in hopes of having your company being determined if ever I was made a fool by

Marriage it should be only on account of the day not the deed.

No tidings coming the 1st of April and being told by Captain of a Sloop that arrived here, that a foreign pidgeon near Busorah (supposed to be a pattamar or packett carrier) was shott by one of the consulls sporting Servants as she was regaling herself in a field of fine corn near the ostrich, which the frenchman shot at and wounded in the thigh, what was only bare sufficient to hurt the Ostrich, was more than enough to kill his companion the poor pidgeon. The smart the large bird felt, his grief for the loss of his guide and by being a stranger to the place occasioned in him so great a pannick that on the violent acuteness of his pain he let fly his charge at the french Man's head thinking thereby at once to be revenged for his cruelty to him and the pidgeon, and returned back again as it is reported, but nobody yet has been able to discover the rout he took. The French man inquisitive to see what that huge Bird had let fly at him took it up, but how great was his surprise when instead of a —— he found a packett directed to Mynheer Vanderdujsen, this he looked on as a lucky omen for France for discovering some plot against the Government on an east India Expedition and sent it with a long relation of Circumstances to the french Consull at Aleppo who forwarded it in State to France as a prize worthy the King his Masters notice.

The loss of my advices was a very great disappointment to me as my hopes of seeing you at Bombay where at an end. Therefore the next day being the 2nd of April I gave my hand and heart to my present Companion for life, its true people may say this comes within the verge of an April day, I sincerely rejoice at being made one of those fools.

I cannot say I have smoaked since I saw you last, but I am never the less obliged to you for your intended present of Tobbaca and pipes, it was more for the sake of stopping your pipe that I relished the smell of Tobbaca, than any real pleasure I enjoyed from its Effluvia. I am sorry you are likely to lose the use of my cousin Betsys little finger by its being worn to the stump, mine should be at your service, but my husband will not part with it, therefore in order to obviate that difficulty I have sent you by my Papa a comical sort of Tobbaca stopper, which I beg may supply the place of my finger. I daresay it will suit your purpose and the donor will be honoured with your acceptance.

There is a brother of my husbands Mr. Thomas Boddam (as arrand a smoaker as ever was) now returning to Europe. He has been long at a subbordinate Factory and is a meer Moorman as to the language taste and customs, and will suck a Hubble Bubble, draw a Ailloon, smoak a hooka or cream-cann with you if you please; he has promised to wait on you with an account of us and to show you his different smoaking Machines being curious that way. he says he makes no doubt to prove to you that his method is the best for tasting the real essence of the Tobacco, their is musick in his smoaking Instruments not unlike croaking of frogs. now I mention musick it recalls to mind your question of myself, and thus I answer it,—My Harpsicord is in good tune and often in practis, I have been told, now dont think me vain, my learning time has not been ill bestowed and that I am a tollerable profficient; I continue to sing as merrily as ever, and think my voice is much improved since I came to India.

Good god Doctor where did you learn that I was grown quite grave. Its true Marriage has made me a little more steady than I was before, but grave I never shall be till I am the mother of a dozen children; I have sence enough to know that too much reserve as too much giddiness are both unbecoming at my years; but to be serious; I am in a fair way to being a mother, or of adding another relation to the family. My sister has shewn me so good an example how could I do otherwise than follow it.

I am now to return you thanks Dear Sir for the receit of the peas pudding you sent me. I had nineteen or twenty of my friends dined with me some time ago, and served that up as one dish, they all tasted of it, and said they never eat anything so fine in all their lives. so much for the honour of your peas pudding. Doctor I am afraid it will be a long time before I have the pleasure of sitting with you by the fire side at St. Sepulchers.

I have taken the liberty to send you a small quantity of Beetle (not Betel) nut of which I beg your acceptance, If it is too much for yourself please to distribute it among your friends and acquaintance and have likewise send you some Chunam which the country people use to make their Lips red. I generally eat some (of) it and rub my cheeks with a course towel before I enter the Ball Room; perhaps you think we have no entertainments or amusements of any kind but give me leave to tell you that Bombay is a little Britan; If I have an opportunity by the next shipping will send you some Bombay Diamonds and other very curios precious stones of my own collecting, for if you remember I was always something of a Vertuoso, and the next ship which my husband sends to the Island of Magadoxa[1] will if possible procure for you a Merman or Maid which you like best.

As for birds of song we have very few here, the only one I have heard the gentlemen commend, are the Tumenekakihas, but as I am not very well acquainted with them. Shall refer you to my Papa. I shall send you a very large Collection of most beautiful Curiosities.

But to be serious I am now going to lose in my Papa the best of friends. Indeed did it not seem a little too selfish could wish his stay much longer but as his return to his native Country is to enjoy the fruits of his labours and compensate his being deprived of the company of his friends that are (near) and dear to him.

I think I have filled up a tollerable quantity of paper, and am sure you will be heartily tired before you have read it thro, so Sir I bid you adieu, and am your affectionate, dutifull, obliged, obedient, humble Servant and Niece

MARY RAWSON HART BODDAM.

" and that his soul in heaven may dwell etc. etc."

In its playful humour this letter of the little child bride has a charm which is peculiarly its own. The writer's ingenuity in devising extraordinary means of

[1] Magadoxo (Mukdishu), a seaport of Italian Somaliland, East Africa: a famous trade centre from the 14th century: wrongly described as an island by Marco Polo.—*Enc. Britannica.*

transit to enable her beloved uncle and aunt to grace her wedding ceremony is especially to be noted. Strangely enough, in her innocent fashion she intelligently anticipated the aerial post of our twentieth century day, tracing out for her flying birds and her flying camels almost the exact route which, in its later stages, the Handley Page aeroplanes followed during their recent historic flight to India.

Mary's allusion to smoking—" I cannot say I have smoaked since I saw you last "—is doubtless only a reply to some chaffing reference of the Vicar's to the smoking habits of Anglo-Indian ladies, and is not to be taken as an indication of the writer's predilection for tobacco at some earlier period. But it is an undoubted fact that smoking was practised in India by English ladies in the eighteenth century. Nor was the smoking medium a delicate cigarette, but that full-blooded instrument of eastern tobacco devotees—the Hooka. This device consists of a bowl in which tobacco reduced to a paste is placed. Attached are long tubes through which the smoke after passing through water is drawn into the lungs by inhalation. The tobacco is usually a mild Persian variety, with its fragrance enhanced by the addition of sweet herbs and spices.

Price, in his *Tracts*, published about the year 1782, mentions that hooka-smoking " is so very pleasant that many ladies take the tube and draw a little of the smoak into their mouths." There are other references to the hooka-smoking of ladies of this period. But it was, of course, amongst the men that the habit was most inveterately practised. Mary's citation of her brother-in-law as " a meer Moorman (Mahommedan)" who "will suck a Hubble Bubble, draw a Ailloon, smoak a hooka or cream-cann with you if you please," is of special interest as a revelation of the wide variety of the instruments of smoking employed by Eastern connoisseurs of the weed and their British imitators. So comprehensive, indeed, were this "meer Moorman's" tastes that it is not at first easy to discover the precise direction in which his smoking habits were exercised.

The Hubble Bubble we know as a popular form of the Hooka—a sort of poor man's pipe in which a section of cocoanut shell takes the place of the costly material of which the bowl of the Hooka is formed, and reeds or other common productions supplant the elegant mouthpieces. But what is an "Ailloon," and still more what is a "Cream Can"? "Hobson-Jobson," that valuable *vade mecum* for the interpretation of quaint or obsolete Anglo-Indian expressions, is silent on the point, and no help is to be obtained from the ordinary Oriental dictionaries.

If, however, we turn to books of Oriental travel pertaining to this period we shall find the solution of the mystery. Edward Ives, who went out to the East with Admiral Watson as surgeon to the flagship, in his work[1] gives an account of a visit to the island of Karec at the head of the Persian Gulf, mentioning how at the house of a European resident he "passed some time very agreeably and smoked the Calloon and Kerim Can pipes" which, he went on to say, "are used by the gentlemen here in the same manner as the Hooka is in Bengal." In a note the author explains that the Kerim Can pipe was so called "from a Persian General of that name who invented it, or, perhaps, from the word Kerim, which, in the Persian language, signifies a horn or tube."

[1] *A Voyage from England to India in the year* 1754, by Edward Ives. London, 1773.

Niebuhr, who visited India in 1764, has also a reference to the popular pipe of the period. " Kerim Kan, the present Shah in the South of Persia," he wrote,[1] " seems to distinguish himself at this amusement (smoking), for the pipe that is most in fashion is called a Kerim-Kan." Niebuhr's explanation is probably the more correct one ; but however that may be the identity of the "Ailloon " and the " Cream Can " of Mary's letter with the Persian pipes of the period is placed beyond dispute.

Some of the other allusions of the writer are deserving of passing notice. The Bombay diamonds spoken of were probably ordinary Indian precious stones. For these, from very early days, Bombay had been a market. The servants of the Company dealt extensively in them as one of the most promising sources of profit open to them. It is on record that Sir Nicholas Waite, the rascally Governor of Bombay, who was deposed by his Council and deported to England in 1711, when searched on arrest had on his person some parcels of diamonds which were the property of the Company. The dissolution of the Mogul Empire then in active progress forced upon the market enormous quantities of precious stones. Moreover, the famous Golconda diamond field had not yet yielded up all its riches.

The Betel nut included in Mary's gifts to her uncle is a familiar object of native domestic use. With the accompanying chunam or lime and catechu it is chewed by Indians of all ages and sexes much as gum is by our Transatlantic cousins. The catechu gives a vermilion stain to the lips resembling the discolourment of blood, hence many visitors on first landing in

[1] *Travels in Egypt, Syria, and Arabia.*

India have been induced to the belief that the people they encountered were suffering from pulmonary hæmorrhage. That in Mary's day the catechu had its uses in the toilet of European ladies is shown by her statement as to its doing duty on occasions for rouge.

Now we must take leave of the sprightly Mary. Unhappily it must be a last farewell, for within eighteen months of penning the letter given above she had passed to the great account. She died soon after the birth of her son Charles Boddam (1762–1811), and was buried in the compound of Bombay Cathedral. Over the grave on the north side of the Cathedral may still be read the inscription placed upon the tombstone by her husband: "Here lies the body of Mary Boddam, wife of Rawson Hart Boddam, who departed this life the 9th day of July Anno Domini 1762, aged 18 years."

Through the second marriage of her youngest sister, Louisa, Eliza was connected with another conspicuous Anglo-Indian in the person of Colonel Charles Pemble, who held high military rank in Western India at a somewhat later period. Louisa's earlier matrimonial venture had been a dire failure. We do not know in what respect the union was unfortunate, but from the tone of the family letters it is clear that she was an object of commiseration. Her marriage to Colonel Pemble, in a worldly sense at all events, was quite satisfactory. In consequence of it Louisa became a *grande dame* in the settlement with an establishment second only to that of the Governor. We shall hear a good deal about her in Eliza's letters which will be given in later pages.

Originally Colonel Pemble was a Bengal officer, one who had fought under Monro at the battle of Buxar and had been transferred to the Western Presidency because of his military experience. If, however, a story which Mr. James Douglas tells in his work on old Bombay[1] is authentic, Pemble lacked the understanding of native character which was one of the sources of the success of Clive and other great Indian commanders. According to this authority Pemble issued an order directing that all native officers should wear boots, a thing which they had never done before. Not only was custom outraged by the edict, but it appeared to the sensitive minds of the sepoy officers that their caste was endangered. After vain protests against the decree they eventually agreed to wear the hated boots. Their submission, however, was accompanied by a declaration that ill fortune would attend their oppressor because of his disregard of their feelings. In three weeks' time the General, as he had now become, was smitten with dropsy and never recovered. Though the fatal attack was the result of a deep-seated disease, native superstition saw in it retribution for the indignity which had been put upon them. Pemble, who was Commander-in-Chief in Western India at the time of his death in 1770, died intestate, and probate was granted to his wife on January 27, 1770–1. Before Louisa became a second time a widow Eliza had passed through the most memorable experiences of her life.

[1] *Bombay and Western India.*

Chapter III

MARRIED LIFE *in* BOMBAY

The Bombay to which Eliza and her sisters returned in 1757 was a pleasant sociable settlement still living under the traditions of the early period of the East India Company's system. But great changes were proceeding, destined ere long to transform the whole edifice of British influence in India. In a few months' time Plassey was to be fought, with all its incalculable consequences for British ascendancy in the East. The struggle between British and French was still going on in Southern India, but three years later the issue was to be finally settled by Sir Eyre Coote's signal victory at Wandewash. Western India was outside the principal theatres upon which the destinies of India were being decided, but it had its own part to play in the drama, and had already played it to a great extent. Its special responsibility was the suppression of the piracy which for generations had constituted a serious impediment to peaceful trading in the Indian Ocean, and had even at times menaced the security of the commercial centres in which the East India Company had interests.

Two distinct groups of pirates operated off the coast of western India in the first half of the eighteenth century. In the north were the Muscateers, as they were termed, Arabs located at Muscat and other Persian Gulf ports, who periodically swept down upon the shipping, trading to Guzerat, leaving a trail of destruction and outrage behind them. They usually gave the well-armed ships of the East India Company a wide berth, but now and again they pounced upon some of the smaller British vessels, carrying off to their lairs in the Gulf such booty as they could seize, and with it the unfortunate British crews of the captured ships, who were condemned in some cases to years of captivity in the Arab states.

Southwards of Bombay, and a more serious menace than the Arabs to commerce because of their proximity to the main centres of the Company's influence and trade, were the Malabar pirates, who owed allegiance to a line of pirate chiefs with the family name of Angria. The first of the dynasty, who came into prominence before the seventeenth century closed, is reputed, before he took up with piracy as a profession, to have been a servant in the household of the Governor of Bombay. He was a resourceful ruffian, and in a few years got about him a miscellaneous force of freebooters who were the terror of the Malabar Coast. His immediate successor, Kanhoji, was even more formidable as a foe of all regular trade. Established in the almost inaccessible mountain fortresses of Severndroog and Gheriah, he maintained at sea regular fleets so strong as to enable him to plunder and levy blackmail almost with impunity. A favourite device of his, as has been stated on an earlier page, was to capture and hold to ransom any Europeans who incautiously ventured within his reach in small or inadequately armed craft. In addition to Mrs. Whitehill, an English merchant named Curnegevan was a conspicuous victim of the pirate. This unfortunate was detained a prisoner from 1726 to 1737, and was only released to die at home from the effects of the hardships to which he was subjected.

With a little energy the East India Company might have suppressed the nuisance, but it shrank from the cost. As an alternative to direct action it established a convoy system and attempted diplomacy. The convoys were successful though very expensive, but the diplomatic efforts of the Company's agents failed miserably. The records amusingly illustrate this.

On one occasion the Bombay Council in a letter read the pirate chief a solemn lecture on the evil of his ways, pointing out not only the gross dishonesty of taking what did not belong to him, but the serious consequences to himself which were likely to attend such action.

Kanhoji, in his reply, was frankly impudent. In sarcastic allusion to the exhortations and arguments in the English letter he observed :

> As touching the desire of possessing what is another's I do not even find the merchants exempt from this sort of ambition, for this is the way of the world, for God gives nothing by favour himself but takes from one to give to another. Whether there is right or no who is able to determine? Your Excellency is pleased to write that he who follows war purely through an inclination that one hath thereto, one time or another will find cause to repent, of which I suppose Your Excellency hath found proof, for we are not always victorious, nor always unfortunate.

In the face of such logic, argument was clearly out of place, and so the Company resigned itself for a good many additional years to the pirate peril. At last the position of affairs became intolerable. Angria's piratical craft practically paralysed local trade. Even the Company's ships were not always exempt from their unwelcome attentions. Foreign rivals of the Company insinuated that the Company tolerated piracy as a cheap and easy method of freeing itself from competition, and there was possibly a grain of truth in the allegation. But with the growing power of the Company it was impossible for the sake of the larger interests which were rapidly growing up to decline the challenge to its prestige which the existence of this predatory power insolently offered. The decision, therefore, was taken to bring to an end the era of coastal anarchy by attacking the pirates in their lairs.

An efficient instrument for the Company's purpose existed in the shape of a well-equipped marine force under the command of a highly capable seaman named William James. James was one of those adventurous spirits who were nurtured in the service of the East India Company. His origin is somewhat obscure, but according to the best authenticated tradition he was born in 1721, the son of a Pembrokeshire miller. In early life he ran away to sea and had an interesting career in the West Indies. In 1747 he entered the East India Company's service and was employed as chief mate, and afterwards as Commander of the *Guardian*, a ship of war belonging to the Bombay Marine. In 1751 he was promoted Commodore and Commander-in-Chief of the Company's marine force, with a broad pennant on the *Protector*, a ship mounting forty-four guns. Under his command the force attained to a high standard of discipline. It was, in fact, a formidable weapon of offence, especially when used against a barbaric foe poorly equipped with cannon and lacking the cohesion which the European system of sea training conferred.

James proved his capacity and the qualities of the Indian Marine in the work which was entrusted to him in 1755 of destroying the pirates' power. Angria's chief stronghold was a great island fortress some distance to the south of Bombay, known as Severndroog, or "the Golden Fortress." Built in the fifteenth century by the Mahommedan Kings of Bijapur, and strengthened in 1660 by the redoubtable Mahratta chief, Sivaji, this place was regarded as impregnable in its early history, and in fact it was so against an Oriental enemy. But Commodore James, with British determination, overcame all the formidable obstacles in his way, and after a sharp bombardment of the fort stormed and captured it in a night attack with the aid of a Mahratta force which operated from the landward side. The pirate chief eluded his grasp, but a great booty fell to him with all the miscellaneous equipment of an Oriental place of arms. It was a brilliant feat, gallantly carried through, but it left the work only half done. There still remained to Angria the sister stronghold of Gheriah on the same coast.

Gheriah had a similar history to that of Severndroog: it was equally formidable in a military sense. Towering high above a convenient little harbour which its guns should have effectively defended, it offered possibilities of successful defence which were not to be ignored. The Company, in framing its measures for the subjection of the fortress, decided to take no risks.

A small but well-armed squadron was despatched from home in 1756 under the command of Admiral Watson to co-operate with the Indian Marine under Commodore James. The charge of the military portion of the expedition was entrusted to Clive, who, though still to fight the battle of Plassey, had already achieved distinction as a soldier. As on the previous occasion, the Mahrattas co-operated on the land side—shifty, unscrupulous allies who in the end were rather a burden than a help in the working out of the plan of campaign. In the result Gheriah, like Severndroog, fell an easy prey to the British forces.

Angria, when he found that the decision was going against him, fled to the Mahratta camp. He afterwards surrendered to the British, and in the end settled down to a retired life as a pensioner of the Company. Again a great booty fell into the hands of the captors. There was no less than £100,000 in silver specie, and probably as much more in valuable effects found in the pirate camp. It was believed at the time that this was only a small part of the pirate store, and that the real hoard of treasure was made over to the Mahrattas by Angria. That would have been quite in keeping with Mahratta traditions and principles. Whether they profited to this large extent is not certain, but they did very well out of the transaction. In the final settlement they got Gheriah itself, giving to the British Government in exchange for it a small territory on the Konkan Coast opposite to Bombay, upon which Fort Victoria was afterwards built.

In accordance with custom, all who participated in the expedition shared in the booty. Commodore James's portion was a substantial one, and, added to his previously-acquired wealth, it enabled him to retire to England in 1758 a rich man. He bought an estate at Eltham, but lived mainly at his residence in Gerard Street, Soho, a thoroughfare already consecrated by great literary memories, and soon to have, through its

SIR WILLIAM JAMES, BT.

association with Sterne and Eliza, another leaf added to its wreath of fame.

James was now an important man in Company circles in England. His personal qualities reinforced his honourable record as a recommendation to the kind of distinction which went with high Indian achievement in those days. He was, above all, genial and companionable, had a great store of interesting reminiscences to draw upon, and, what was perhaps most important in a host, had the gift of making friends amongst a class whose distinction was intellectual rather than social. A varied and interesting circle of guests soon gathered about him. In some way or other Sterne became a frequent and honoured visitor. From the rooms the novelist then occupied in Bond Street he almost daily walked across to Gerard Street to spend some time with the James's. Later he met there Eliza. But before we describe the circumstances which brought about this strange association we must give a few details bearing upon Eliza's history prior to her second departure for England.

Eliza's earliest married years, if not spent happily, were free of any serious disagreements or misunderstandings. She became the mother of two children in this period. There was first a boy, who was born in 1759 and died ten years later at his grandfather Thomas Whitehill's house at Worfield in Shropshire; and then a girl, Elizabeth, born in 1761, who on October 1, 1785, married Thomas Nevill, by whom she had one son and three daughters. Eliza's domestic cares must have occupied most of her attention, and that these weighed somewhat unduly upon her may be gathered from the tenour of her letters. The first of her communications, figuring in a fragmentary form as No. 2 of Lord Basing's collection, is addressed to Miss Elizabeth Sclater and dated Bombay 26 Sept., 1762. Though written in a playful, ironic style, it conveys an underlying sense of the burdens of motherhood experienced by this young girl yet in her teens.

In its incomplete form the letter is as follows:

. . . Majesties subjects in India which if he by weighty arguments brings to effect we shall have cause to bless him and he will in some measure have attoned for his former remissness—it is that he should petition the parliament for every married man who introduced a subject into the World once a year, to live tax free, in all parts of the Kings Dominions, it would encourage many poor persons to Wedlock, who now are frighted at the thoughts of a Family, and the poor are certainly the most useful people in the procreation way as experience shows us every day by the number of stout seamen and soldiers they supply the nation with.

I leave it to him whether such a scheme would not be of general utility to all degrees of Men, therefore if he joins in my opinion we may one day hope to see it take place and hope he will not take all the merit of it to himself but allow me the credit of having been projector. probably then Draper may think of settling in his native Country, otherwise he must be contented with revisiting it for one twelvemonth and return to pass the remainder of our days at Bombay (if we continue to increase and multiply as we have done) unless dame fortune should be particularly lavish of her favours to us, which dependance is too precarious for reasonable Souls to have any faith in,—

I really my dear Cousin am so much altered with breeding, suckling and other dangerous illnesses, that I appear ten years older than I am, nor do I believe you will know me again if I return to England with Mr. Draper after Christmas, When I left London I was fat and rosy but now I am quite the reverse, yet my spirits are good as ever, and till they subside, I shall not give myself up for lost.

You, if I remember right, Betsy, used to be troubled with fits, I hope they have now left you, for indeed companions of such a nature are dreadful underminers of a good constitution, as I from fatal experience have great cause to vouch ; I have not had the pleasure of hearing from your Brother more than once since I have been in India, though I have wrote him two letters, as probably a female correspondence may be thought too great a condescension from him to me, I shall not trouble him with repetitions of it till I hear from himself it is otherwise.

Pray present my best wishes and respects to him, Mr. Mrs. & the Miss Hillersdons. Sophia now I imagine is grown a fine young Lady, and perhaps Mr. Thomas Sclater's favourite toast ; the small remains of my paper reminds me it is time to make an end of scribbling which I will do after assuring you dear Cousin I am very affectionately hers, unfeignedly

E. DRAPER.

BOMBAY Sep the 26th 1762
To Miss ELIZABETH SCLATER

Another letter, undated, but probably also belonging to 1762, was addressed to Mrs. Pickering, wife of the Vicar of St. Sepulchre's :

[Date about 1762.]

MY dear Aunt Pickering's obliging favour I had the pleasure to receive, it was a most welcome one, though in the chiding strain. She complains that I write but seldom and my letters are short. I wish I had not reason to accuse her of the same defect in hers. You say Madam that you must write to my Sister which prevents your writing me so much as you otherwise would. Was I, my dear Aunt, to make the same excuse I should not (by your rule) write above two lines to each of my friends. For I have upwards of twenty letters to answer by every Conveyance, besides duplicates.

I imagine you must have heard that poor Polly is no more. Never was young person so much altered in disposition as she was the last year of her life ; from one of the most gay lively spirited Girls in the World she was become one of the most melancholy, constantly in tears, and saying she should die, she never was easy till she was with child, and always unhappy afterwards. the silent grief which she took a pleasure in indulging, certainly preyed on her spirits, and brought on her untimely end. Such Madame was the death of one of the finest Girls India ever produced. she was generally beloved and of course universally lamented ; the tenth day after her labour she expired very suddenly in Convulsions. Her little boy is extremely like her and doated on by his poor Father on that account.

I certain Madam shall have the pleasure of seeing you in England in twelvemonths, when I hope to make myself as agreable to my friends, as you kindly prognosticate. I shall be very happy if I can present my little boy and girl to you. the former is just recovered from the small pox and the latter a most sweet baby.

I do not recolect Miss Snelgrove but am much obliged for her kind enquiries and good wishes. Pray, Madam please to present my duty to my Aunt Loyd I would write to her but am incapable of amusing her therefore hope she will excuse me till I can pay her my personal compliments. Adieu my ever dear Madame and believe till I have the pleasure of seeing you, that I am with duty, love and gratitude

Your obliged Niece

ELIZA DRAPER.

Though its interest is almost entirely domestic, this letter is valuable from the light it throws on Eliza's character. The reference to " poor Polly "—her sister Mary—is charged with true affection, and gives a quite pathetic picture of the last days of that sprightly little lady who in the letter given on an earlier page repudiated with such amusing warmth the charge that she had " grown quite grave." The woman speaks out, too, in Eliza's allusions to her children. Only a good mother could thus have written. One of the little ones, the boy, it may be noted, had just recovered from small-pox. The disease at that time was far more dreaded than it is to-day, when vaccination has so largely mitigated its consequences. In India it claimed many victims. Indeed, it was seldom absent from the towns and villages.

The Indians of that day had a curious method of treating small-pox, which is described in Ives's work previously mentioned. It seems that on the capture of Gheriah two of Angria's children were found suffering from the disease. Ives, as the Admiral's medical attendant, treated them, sending them such medicines as he thought proper. "They always appeared very thankful for what I did," observed Ives, "but I afterwards discovered that they had not taken any of the medicines. They preferred the common method used by the physical practitioners in their country, besprinkling the patient with sifted wood ashes as soon as the postules began to fill, which they add to or diminish from according to the greater or less quantity of variolous matter. One of his family had a pock of the confluent kind and was covered from head to foot with ashes, which, towards the latter end of the disorder, appeared like a mass of paste surrounding the whole body. The whole family of Angria recovered, however, from the disease."

There was no doubt a powerful antiseptic quality in the wood ashes. The Indian cure, therefore, was not without its strong merits, especially in those backward days of Western medical science.

In the letter given above Eliza clearly intimated the

possibility of her early departure from India on a visit to her English relations. But more than two years must have elapsed after the writing of this communication before the visit was actually paid. There is an unfortunate hiatus in the correspondence at this juncture which prevents us from following with any particularity the doings of Eliza. All that we know is that her husband's nervous malady increased to such an extent that he was compelled to take a trip to England in the hope of relief. No doubt the desirability of placing the two children out at school also weighed with the parents. We do not hear of them again until the couple have been some little time in England. Then they are revealed—Draper taking the waters at some Spa with little benefit to his complaint, and Eliza visiting her friends and enjoying life but indifferently well owing to the sickness of her children.

What we know of their doings in this period is disclosed in this fragment of a letter (No. 4 of Lord Basing's collection) addressed to Miss Elizabeth Sclater at Messrs. Sclater and Sheppard's, in Newgate Street, London. The letter is not dated, but appears to have been written in 1765 or 1766 :

. . . you Betsey under the seal of secrecy. Therefore hope you will not divulge any part of this letter, because my sentiments are not calculated at present for any but friendly inspection, and the knowledge of them would only occasion my poor sister's misfortune to be more generally known. We continued a day at Worcester in our journey to Worfield where I visited Mrs. Sclater, who behaved with her usual complaisance ; her daughter was at home and is, I think, one of the finest Young Creatures I ever beheld. She was particular in her enquiries after yourself and family. Many compliments passed between us before I took my leave.

Mr. Draper has not yet received any benefit from the . . . borough Waters, but I am in hopes his next letter will contain such wished for intelligence. My young family are in a very indifferent way, confined to their Apartment; what with sickness and vexation I am really an object of pity. My Uncle Joseph dined here on Friday (He) seemed cheerful and well.

You are a very execrable flatterer Betsy, therefore do not attempt to compliment me a second time. It is too luscious a food to be swallowed greedily without cloying. I believe I have received my share of it for I do not find it so agreable to my taste now as it formally used to be. If I was not to introduce something bordering on the whimsical you would scarcely know this letter for mine though signed by the hand of your affectionate

ELIZA DRAPER.

Duty and compts attend the Family at Chingford.

The Mrs. Sclater referred to in the letter was the second wife (Miss Penelope Lutley) of Richard Sclater (1711–1754), and lived at the Tythings, near Worcester. She was Eliza's aunt, and her daughter was Miss Penelope Lutley (1752–1843), who died unmarried. Worfield, mentioned by Eliza, was near Bridgnorth in Shropshire, and the home of Charles Whitehill, who lived there till 1788.

Up to the point at which the narrative has arrived nothing has occurred to indicate that Eliza's marriage had been other than a happy one. Her reference to Draper in the epistle just quoted, though not excessively affectionate, is quite in keeping with the theory of perfectly harmonious relations between the two. There is certainly no suggestion of the existence of an unbearable yoke impatiently submitted to—the position which afterwards developed. We have to remember, however, that Eliza was still a mere child in years. Moreover, though she was of precocious intelligence, she lacked that complete knowledge of the world which was essential to her full development. There was now opening to her a new life in which her natural gifts would be quickened by contact with one of the greatest intellects of the time.

Chapter IV

INTIMACY *with* STERNE

The crisis in Eliza's life now approaches. Draper, in or about 1765, returned to India to renew his official life. Appointed Accountant-General shortly after his arrival, we soon see him immersed in his work and conducting a bitter controversy with Hornby, a Member in Council and subsequent Governor of Bombay, over some stores which the latter is alleged to have misappropriated. Meanwhile, Eliza, freed from family cares by the departure of her husband and the placing of her children out at school at Salt Hill, is enjoying life after her own fashion. Flitting about from one pleasant country residence to another she agreeably passes her time. Hoddington, of course, claims her. Her best of friends cousin Elizabeth, and her more than friend cousin Tom, are always ready to welcome her. In their society she almost forgets that she has ever been away. Girlish still, in spite of her matronhood, she carols joyfully through the woods and green fields of pleasant Hampshire, revelling in the pure delights of what is for her God's own country.

If the truth were known, these were probably the golden days of her life. Never afterwards was she able to recapture the rapturous thrill of that period with all its joyous experiences and its memories of sweet companionship. Let the reader note in the correspondence presently to be introduced how Eliza dwells upon her recollection of this past—how earnestly she longs for the old life within sound of

> The bells of sweet St. Mary's
> On fair English ground.

When the winter came Eliza moved to London to spend some time with her friends the James's at their house in Soho. There we find her in the early days of January 1767, an intimate of Mrs. James, and a welcome addition to the circle over which that lady presides.

Fate plays some strange tricks with the association of individuals, but rarely has it fashioned a more curious link than that which connects Laurence Sterne and Elizabeth Draper. There was a remarkable, even a striking, contrast between the two: Sterne, well advanced in years and older in feelings, stricken as to health and cynical as to disposition, and as a man soured and disappointed by the buffetings of a not ill-deserved fate ; Eliza, young (she was only 22) and attractive, vivacious to a degree, talented and instinct with the indefinable charm of the true feminine. You might at the time have searched London society from end to end without finding two more opposite types. Yet they came together almost instantly on meeting in Mrs. James's drawing-room. We may suspect that the pace was forced by Sterne, who had a constitutional weakness for a pretty face and an elegant figure.

Whatever the truth, the novelist's fancy was instantly caught by this bright little woman whose graceful girlish figure and animated face offered so piquant a contrast to the stiff, artificial fashionable lady of the day. What he saw in her is best told in his own words, contained in a letter written when the acquaintance had well ripened :

> You are not handsome, Eliza, nor is yours a face that will please a tenth part of your beholders—but are something more; for I scruple not to tell you, I never saw so intelligent, so animated, so good a countenance. . . . A something in your eyes, and voice, you possess is a degree more persuasive than any woman I ever saw, read, or heard of. . . . Your eyes, and the shape of your face (the latter the most perfect oval I ever saw) which are perfections that must strike the most indifferent judge.

Though this vividly sketched picture may be accepted in all its details as a faithful presentment of Eliza, it is, unfortunately, not possible to compare it with any portrait.[1] Several are known to have been painted at Sterne's request, notably a beautiful miniature by Cosway showing Eliza divested of her ornaments and in simple vestal garb, but protracted inquiry has failed to reveal their whereabouts, though probably they still exist in some collection of unnamed subjects.

How speedily the acquaintance of the two ripened is shown in the literary memorials of Sterne. They met frequently on an easy footing. Almost every day communications passed between them. So far had things advanced within the first fortnight that Sterne was sending Eliza a complete set of his works with the following characteristic letter :

> ELIZA will receive my books with this—the Sermons came all hot from the heart—I wish that could give em any title, to be offer'd to Mrs. . . . the Others came from the head . . . I'm more indifferent abt. their Reception . . .
>
> I know not how it comes in . . . but I'm half in love

[1] The portrait forming the frontispiece is of doubtful authenticity.

with you. . . . I ought to be wholly so—for I never valued, (or saw more good Qualities to value) . . . or thought more of one of Yr. Sex than of You. So adieu

Yrs. faithfully if not afftly.

L. STERNE.

Eliza's self-esteem was flattered by the marked attentions of which she was the object. Sterne was then at the height of his fame. *The Sentimental Journey* had still to be born, but *Tristram Shandy* was already a classic, and Uncle Toby and Widow Wadman enjoyed a popularity which made them almost national characters. Quick in intelligence and with natural literary leanings, Eliza would not have been herself if she had felt otherwise than gratified at the novelist's notice. Her response to his overtures was made in the form which appealed most to his whimsical spirit. He, Yorick, "the mild, generous, and good," was her "Bramin," at whose feet she sat to learn wisdom. Not to be outdone in complimentary imagery, Sterne styled Eliza his "Bramine." He probably liked to picture her, his disconsolate widow, immolating herself upon his funeral pyre in the truest Brahminical spirit of affection and submission.

Mrs. James, a pleasant, comfortable type of woman, not overburdened with respect for conventions, appears to have looked on at this queer friendship with complacency, if not with distinct approval. Sometimes she accompanied Eliza on her visits to Sterne; also, she shared in their amusements and excursions. Indeed, so far as she was concerned, the whole connection was on a basis which admitted of no question—or at least required no defence. Her judgment may have been obscured by the glamour of Sterne's genius. It was no small thing for a woman of her social aspirations to have under her control so very considerable a lion as the novelist then was. But it cannot be imagined that she would have allowed herself to become a victim of any such weakness if real cause had existed for censure.

In assessing the character of the relations which existed between Eliza and Sterne it seems that the friendly attitude maintained towards the intimacy by Mrs. James is of great importance. It is not, of course, conclusive of the innocency of the acquaintance, but it does throw a distinctly favourable light upon it. More convincing, however, even than Mrs. James's patronage of the friendship is Eliza's own action at this period. So little care did she take to conceal the advances of Sterne that she actually sent a copy of Sterne's letter printed above to her cousin Thomas Limbrey Sclater. If an irrevocable step had really been taken her cousin would have been about the last repository of her confidences. Assuming, however, that the whole affair was a mere flirtation, we can imagine the spirit which would prompt Eliza to confide to her old comrade the secrets of her adventure. It would pique him, cast a reflection on his own laggard and, in a sentimental sense, inadequate epistolary efforts, and it might enhance his estimate of the worth of his cousin to know that she was the object of so much devotion at the hands of a man with whose fame the whole country was ringing.

That Eliza's feelings were stirred any more deeply than friendship allows is contrary to the whole tenour of the facts as they are revealed in the correspondence. When Sterne sent her his portrait in exchange for her own she flattered him by placing it over her writing-table, but it was a mere exaggerated courtesy dictated probably by gratitude for the novelist's solicitude for her intellectual advancement. He had, or he professed to have, a high admiration for her literary ability. "Who taught you the art of writing so sweetly, Eliza?" he asked on one occasion, and added, "You have absolutely exalted it to a science." Sterne proclaimed Eliza as a newly arrived genius to his friends in society. On one occasion he sounded her praises so eloquently that Lord Bathurst, with whom he was dining, toasted her health on three separate occasions.

The pleasant companionship received a rude shock when, early in the spring, a letter arrived from Draper practically commanding his wife to rejoin him in India. Eliza was terribly upset at the communication. She dreaded this return to the old depressing life of Bombay with its dull round of duties with a man whose nature was so out of sympathy with her own. In her distress she became really ill and took to her bed. Sterne, on calling at Gerard Street one morning, for the first time found the presence of his fair friend denied to him. He took his discomfiture very badly. He could not sleep that night, and when morning came he wrote this letter expostulating with Eliza on her cruelty: "Remember, my dear, that a friend has the same right as a physician. The etiquette of this town (you'll say) otherwise—— No matter! Delicacy and propriety do not always consist in observing their frigid doctrines."

Moved by the appeal, Eliza relented, and Sterne became a daily visitor in her sickroom. She was really ill, and at one time her condition caused anxiety. Sterne, ever susceptible, yielded to the influence of the adverse change in the patient by composing an epitaph on her which he transmitted to his daughter, Lydia, in a letter thoroughly typical of the writer. Referring to

Eliza, he wrote: "She has a tender frame and looks like a drooping lily, for the roses are fled from her cheeks—I can never see or talk to this incomparable woman without bursting into tears. I have a thousand obligations to her, and I owe her more than her whole sex, if not all the world put together. She has a delicacy in her way of thinking that few possess. Our conversations are of the most interesting nature and she talks to me of quitting the world with more composure than others think of living in it. I have wrote an epitaph of which I send thee a copy—'Tis expressive of her modest worth—but may heaven restore her! May she live to write mine!

Columns and labour'd urns but vainly shew
An idle scene of decorated woe:
The sweet companion and the friend sincere
Need no mechanic help to force the tear.

In heartfelt numbers, never meant to shine,
'Twill flow eternal o'er a hearse like thine;
'Twill flow while gentle goodness has one friend
Or kindred tempers have a tear to lend."

The novelist's elegiac efforts were premature. Eliza, under the competent care of Mrs. James, soon recovered sufficiently to leave her bed. But as the time approached for her departure she had a relapse, due probably to worry at the contemplation of her future. Sterne, taking this depression as an indication of sorrow at their coming separation, strongly urged Eliza to put off all thoughts of returning to India. "Write to your husband," he said; "tell him the truth in your case. If he is the generous, humane man you describe him to be, he cannot but applaud your conduct." Sterne went on to offer to bear Eliza's expenses during another year in England and to sequester his livings if necessary for the purpose, for, he said, he could not bear to see Eliza "sacrificed for the paltry consideration of a few hundreds." Finally, the writer suggested that should Mrs. Draper wish it he could summon his wife and daughter to London in order that they might take her to their home in the South of France, where he would join them for a winter in Florence and Naples.

There was too much common sense in Eliza's composition for her to be beguiled by this wild offer. She put it firmly aside and steadily made her preparations for departure. When Sterne found that he could not divert her from her purpose he reluctantly abandoned his plan. But it was with a heavy heart that he took leave of Eliza. In one of his letters he describes how, having handed Eliza into the chaise which was to take her to Deal, where she was for some days to await embarkation on the East Indiaman, he returned to his lodgings in anguish of spirit. He had long suffered from hæmorrhage of the lungs, and that night a new attack came on. In his delirium he fancied that Eliza returned just as he was dying, clasped his hands, and raising her fine eyes bade him be of comfort. Recovering somewhat, he sent a daily letter to Eliza directing her movements and making arrangements for her comfort. We may quote No. IV of the printed series :

To whom should Eliza apply in her distress but to a friend who loves her. Your piano forte must be tuned from the brass middle string of your guitar, which is C. I have got you a hammer too, and a pair of plyers to twist your wire with, and may every one of them, my dear, vibrate sweet comfort to my hopes ! I have bought you ten handsome brass screws, to hang your necessaries upon : I purchased twelve, but stole a couple from you to put in my own cabin at Coxwould—I shall never hang, or take my hat off one of them, but I shall think of you. I have written, also to Mr. Abraham Walker Pilot, at Deal, that I had dispatched these in a packet, directed to his care; which I desired he would seek after, the moment the Deal machine arrived. I have moreover, given him directions, what sort of armchair you would want, and have directed him to purchase the best that Deal could afford, and take it, with the parcel, in the first boat that went off.

In another letter he condoles with her on her cabin being repainted, and fears that it will make her ill, and asks her to be very careful and not run any risk. In the ninth letter he writes:

Talking of widows—pray Eliza, if ever you are such, do not think of giving yourself to some wealthy nabob—because I design to marry you myself. My wife cannot live long—she has sold all the provinces in France already—and I know not the woman I should like so well for her substitute as yourself. It is true, I am ninety-five in constitution, and you but twenty-five—rather too great a disparity this!—but what I want in youth I will make up in wit and good humour—Not Swift so loved Stella, Scarron his Maintenon or Waller his Sacharissa, as I will love, and sing thee, my wife elect!

Sterne's last words of parting in one of these letters show the workings of his tortured soul in these, for him, days of stress and trial. After a caution as to the intimacies she might form on shipboard he wrote:

Best of God's works, farewell! Love me, I beseech thee, and remember me for ever! x x x Adieu! Adieu! and with my adieu let me give thee one streight rule of conduct that thou hast heard from my lips in a thousand forms—but I concenter it in one word Reverence thyself! x x Blessings, rest and Hygeia go with thee! Mayst thou soon return in peace and affluence to illumine my night! I am and shall be the last to deplore thy loss and will be the first to greet and hail thy return.

The East Indiaman, the *Earl of Chatham*, with Eliza on board, sailed from the Downs on Wednesday, April 3, 1767. In grief at her departure Sterne turned for consolation to his daughter. He exhorted her in anguished terms to go to him to console his lonely existence now that his " dear friend " had left. " For God's Sake persuade (thy mother)," he said, " to come and fix in England. I want thee near me, thou child and darling of my heart."

The summons met with no response until some time later, and the wretched man to occupy his mind turned his attention to the completion of *The Sentimental Journey*, which he had frequently discussed with Eliza, and which undoubtedly owed a great deal of its inspiration to their association.

Another source of consolation was found in the writing of a journal which he and Eliza had agreed to keep in which their feelings and sentiments were to be recorded for mutual edification. The first part of this journal had been sent to Eliza before she sailed from the Downs, and a second instalment up to April 13 had later been despatched to Bombay in the care of a Mr. Watts.

The extant portion from the 13th of April to the 4th of August is now in the British Museum (Addt. MSS. 34527, *pp*. 1–40), and has had a curious history. It is probable that after Sterne's death the MSS. passed into the possession of the James's, as when it came to light there were with it two letters from Sterne to the James's, a long letter from Eliza addressed to Mrs. James from Bombay (*see* p. 136), and an unfinished draft of a letter from Sterne to Daniel Draper. All these manuscripts were acquired by a Mr. Gibbs, of Bath, and after his death drifted with other old papers and documents to an attic in the house. When playing in the room one day Mr. Gibbs's son, Thomas Washbourne Gibbs, though only seven years old, found and recognized the papers as something of value, and kept them till his death in 1894, when they passed under his will into the possession of the British Museum.

Sterne was busy writing *The Sentimental Journey* all the summer following Eliza's departure. He had told Eliza in a letter transmitted to Deal that he would freely give her husband five hundred pounds (if money could purchase the privilege) " to let you only sit by me two hours in a day while I wrote my *Sentimental Journey*. I am sure (he added) the work would sell so much the better for it that I should be reimbursed the sum more than seven times told."

This longing for the presence of Eliza grew almost into a possession as time went by. " I have you ever in my mind," he wrote, " and in proportion as I am thus torn from your embraces—*I cling closer to the idea of you*. Your figure is ever before my eyes—the sound of your voice vibrates with its sweetest tones the livelong day in my ear. I can see and hear nothing but my Eliza." On another occasion Sterne describes how while engaged in his study writing *The Sentimental Journey* he dozed off, saw and conversed with Eliza, and then, awaking, found his cat sitting purring contentedly on his knee. There is ample evidence in the personal records of these last days of Sterne of " a mind diseased." Only such could have conceived the terms of a draft letter to Mr. Draper found among his papers, in which he confessed his feelings for Eliza in these terms : " I feel in love with your wife—but 'tis a love you would honour me for—for 'tis so like that I bear my own daughter, who is a good creature, that I scarce distinguish a difference betwixt it."

When Sterne received the first part of Eliza's journal he shut himself in his room, denied himself to all callers, and spent the whole evening and until dinner the next day in reading over and over again the " most interesting account and the most endearing one that ever tried the tenderness of man." " I read and wept and wept and read till I was blind," wrote Sterne in his journal, " then grew sick and went to bed—and in an hour call'd again for the candle—O my Eliza ! thou writest to me with an Angel's pen, and this would win me by thy letters had I never seen thy face or known thy heart."

Early in 1768 Sterne repaired to London with the MS. of *The Sentimental Journey*, and the work was published by Becket on February 25 or 26. The novelist was then, though at the time he was not aware of the fact, in the last stages of his consumptive malady. Eliza was as dominant as ever in his mind. He met Mrs. James, and they wept together in melancholy contemplation of the cruel situation in which two lovers were placed by the decrees of a hard fate. Plans were discussed for a future reunion, in regard to which, if Sterne is to be believed, Mrs. James was quite as eager as himself. Probably he misconstrued a natural pity for the weakness, mental and physical, of an obviously dying man into a cordial endorsement of his wild plans. It mattered little, anyway, what anyone thought or said about them. In a few weeks Sterne was lying dead in his lonely lodgings in Bond Street. His final illness was brought about by his folly in exposing himself to the fatigues of social gatherings when his constitution was in urgent need of rest. But it is scarcely

(By permission of Messrs. W. H. Mansell & Co.)

LAWRENCE STERNE

to be doubted that the depression caused by his separation from Eliza had its own part in accelerating the end.

How Sterne viewed the intimacy which existed between him and Eliza is shown in these curious passages, written in reference to episodes illustrative of their attachment in *The Sentimental Journey*:

> I have brought your name, Eliza, and picture into my work—where they will remain when you and I are at rest for ever.—Some annotater or explainer of my works in this place will take occasion to speak of the friendship which subsisted so long and faithfully betwixt Yorick and the Lady he speaks of—her name he will tell the world—was Draper—a native of India—married there to a gentleman in the India service of that name—who brought her over to England for the recovery of her health in the year '65 where she continued to April the year 1767. It was about three months before her return to India that our author's acquaintance and her's began. Mrs. Draper had a great thirst for knowledge—was handsome, genteel, engaging, and of such gentle dispositions and so enlightened an understanding, that Yorick (whether he made much opposition is not known) from an acquaintance soon became her admirer. They caught fire at each other at the same time, and they would often say without reserve to the world and without any idea of seeing wrong in it, that their affections for each other were *unbounded.* Mr. Draper dying in the year . . . this lady returned to England and Yorick the year after becoming a widower—they were married—and retiring to one of his livings in Yorkshire, where was a most romantic situation—they lived and died happily—and are spoken of with honour in the parish to this day.

In this phantasy we have probably a faithful picture of Sterne's views of his relations with Eliza. There is nothing in what he states to alter the conviction that Eliza's conduct, if highly indiscreet, was not of a guilty complexion. The "unbounded" character of their affection is almost plainly an exaggeration of Sterne's. "Unbounded" affection between two people separated by married ties is not to be proclaimed to the world without provoking social ostracism. Sterne was a fribble and a philanderer, and he seems to have been caught here in his own toils for once. That his sufferings were genuine we have no reason to doubt. What we may seriously question is whether there was ever any real reciprocity. Eliza admired him as a man of genius, had high respect for his understanding, and was grateful to him for the efforts he made to promote her intellectual development. But that was about all. When she set her foot on board the *Earl of Chatham* she had merely a pleasing memory of a charming intellectual companionship. Before the vessel reached Bombay even that memory had grown dim.

Chapter V

ELIZA *rejoins her* HUSBAND

While Sterne, steeped in gloom, was living his last days in a very agony of spirit at the severance of familiar ties Eliza was pursuing the even tenour of her way, enjoying life as an attractive woman may on board ship in the close association of a long voyage. With her had gone out as cabin companion a Miss Hester Light, the destined bride of Mr. George Stretton, or Stratton, a rising man in the Madras branch of the Company's service. This lady appears to have made a pleasing impression upon Eliza. Talented and good-looking, she was one of a class of well-born English girls who in the eighteenth century willingly found their fate in India.[1] She stepped as to the manner born into a position of high influence in Madras, and was a participator, as a spectator, if she was not more actively concerned, in some of the stirring events in which her husband was involved in circumstances to be related.

It is worthy of note that in 1765 Francis Light, the founder of Penang—one of the greatest of the race of Empire builders—had gone out to Bombay as a

[1] The following letter from Mary Harcourt to her brother Lee Harcourt at Madras of December 11, 1720–1, given in one of the volumes of the Historical Manuscripts Commission, may appropriately be cited on this point:

"I receive my dear brother's letter with abundance of satisfaction and perews it often with great deall of pleasure . . . I often fancy myself a setting out for ye East Indies and I believe a small incorridgment would induse me to it. Against I come be sure to look out sharpe for too or three good matches for I desire to bring some young ladys with me."

Volunteer on board one of the ships of the East India Company's marine, and that somewhat later he had settled at Madras with the object of prosecuting private trading with the Malay States. There is nothing to show that Miss Light was related to Francis Light in any way, but it is at least a curious coincidence that the two should be found at Madras in the same period, both just entering upon an Indian career.

More than nine months were occupied by the *Earl of Chatham's* voyage to India. The vessel called, as was then the custom of ships bound for India, at St. Jago, or Santiago, in the Cape Verde Islands. "The vilest spot of earth I ever saw inhabited" was Eliza's description of it. James Forbes, who went out to India two years earlier, was more complimentary when he spoke of the place. Though he found little to attract in the manners of the Portuguese, he and his youthful companions were charmed with a beautiful valley below the town of Porto Praya, which they daily visited to regale on the plantains, cocoanuts, and pineapples with which it abounded. Nowadays, save for an occasional yacht or tramp steamer, Porto Praya is unvisited by British shipping. A dreary, desolate port—a town of tumble-down buildings enclosed by barren hills—it is quite one of the backwaters of modern commerce.

After leaving St. Jago, probably when in the region of the Doldrums, the *Earl of Chatham* encountered a homeward-bound Dutch vessel and transferred to it her mail, which included the second part of Eliza's journal. Afterwards there was no further communication with the outside world until the outgoing ship made her first call in India, probably at Madras. The opportunity thus afforded of sending home letters was availed of by Eliza to address to her cousin, Thomas Limbrey Sclater, a letter supplementing one she had previously forwarded to him from St. Jago. These two communications (Nos. 5 and 6 of Lord Basing's collection) may be introduced here as valuable aids to an understanding of Eliza's character. Take the first as an index to her moods:

FROM the vilest Spot of earth I ever saw & inhabited by the ugliest of Beings—I greet my beloved Cousin —St. Jago the Place—a Charming passage to it. fair winds and fine Weather all the way.—Health too, my friend, is once more return'd to her enthusiastic Votary. I am all life and air and spirits—who'd have thought it, considering me in the light of an Exile—and how do you my Sclater? and how sat the thoughts of my departure on your eyes? and how the reality of it? I want you to answer me a thousand questions—yet hope not of an answer to them for many many months.—I am agreably situated with regard to a Captain—he is polite worthy and good humoured—the officers . . . but Miss Light my associate and Ship Mate (the latter of course if she is the former) very pretty—well behaved and sensible, so that I hope to be as happy as it is possible for a person so circumstanced to be. Did you receive a letter I wrote you from the Downs with a copy of one inclosed from Sterne to me with his sermons and Shandy? I sent such to you.—

Notwithstanding the Bagatelle air I give myself my heart heaves with sighs and my eyes betray its agitating Emotions, every time I think of England and my valuable Connections there—ah my Sclater I almost wish, I had not revisited that Charming Country, or that it had been my fate, to have resided in it for ever—but in the first Instance, the Lords Will has been done—mine I hope may be accomplished in the second.

How do you go on with your Savages? rail not at me for styling them such, because they are not so by profession—believe me, a natural Character of that sort is infinitely worse than a profess'd one.—Are you and Harcourt friends?—

what the Deuce could you be cool or formal about? Men friends to Men—believe me I laugh as much at the Idea of it when their interest comes in competition—as I should at a couple of females swearing unalterable amity and good Will in ernest, on A Pyramid of Glass—till the fabrick (brittle as their friendship) was broke—how long think you it would stand, if a pretty fellow (which they both liked) was to intervene, and tell each fair that the price of his vows was the Demolition of the sacred or sarcastic Alter?—think you both Helens would not endeavour to win a Paris by such a sacrifice—believe me they would—and ridicule not the Policy of our sex—we give up friends to lovers 'tis true—but you give them to things inanimate—for Money or dirty Earth will at any time purchase them of ye—such sordid Wretches ye are.—When I consider ye in that Miserly light I hate ye all, ye all.—

I have nothing more to say, I have no news to send but that you shall hear from me whenever I have an opportunity. That is no news neither—nor is it a compliment—for I love ye so well, that I should debar myself of a pleasure if I refrained from it & that you know—if you've any faith in my sincerity. Adieu my Sclater—Merry be your Heart—and health, love and a competence your portion and I am, and ever shall be y'r affectionate

Eliza Draper.

Earl Chatham 2d May 1767.

Here we find Eliza "all life and spirits," though little more than a month has elapsed since she had parted with Sterne. "How sat the thought of my departure on your eyes?" she asks, but the eyes which concern her are not the novelist's but those of her cousin. Sterne, it is true, is not forgotten, but it is more than doubtful whether he has any considerable share in the "heart heaves" and sighs and "agitating emotions" which are provoked every time she thinks of England. What she most regrets would appear to be the loss of the life of freedom she enjoyed there with its intimacies, not the least treasured of which was that in which her cousin—" my Sclater "—shared. The playful vein in which she rallies Thomas Limbrey Sclater on his friendships is of itself an indication of the main drift of her thoughts. It is just the kind of badinage which would be indulged in by a lively woman at the expense of one who was very near and dear to her. The whole letter, apart from its revelations of feeling, is valuable as an example of Eliza's literary gifts. There is a verve and sparkle in its terse sentences, and a display of true wit in her treatment of her subjects, which support the high opinion Sterne entertained of her epistolary gifts.

The second letter, though in a slightly more subdued vein, is not less delightful as a specimen of good letter writing :

MALLABAR COAST *Earl of Chatham*
29th November 1767.

I WRITE to you from the Element that is supposed to have given birth to our Goddess—does not the prefacing of my letter in this Style give you high notions of my Erudition my Dear Cousin? I am sure it must for I am charm'd with the Brilliancy of the Thought myself upon a reperusal of it; for you cannot suppose that once reading it satisfied me. Oh! you have no Ideas to conceive how wonderfully I am improved—Belle Indian every where—positively 'tis too much. I shall grow vain—then I lose half my excellence which consists in the prettiest decent sort of humility you ever was a witness of.

I sometimes fancy there's a similitude between me and Saint Paul—now will I give you half a Day to find out in what particular thou sad Dull-organized Creature—not instantly to suppose that I mean in point of Eloquence. Take my word for it Cousin that he was as pretty a Gentleman as any you'l find or hear of in the present race of Worthies & scarcely made more Converts to Christianity, than I do to Paganism. Do you wonder at the influence of so engaging a

Deity? I really think (modestly speaking) that its a proof the inhabitants of this section of the Globe possess a something like taste which I fear the poor *Salamanders* knew nothing of. You must suppose (if you've read the *Spectator*, if you have not, I wish you would) I allude to the Women by such an expression as to the other sex, I look upon all of 'em as my own, that I chuse to single out, either for puppets, danglers, or prattlers.

It is six Weeks since I left Miss Light (dear sweet girl) and Madrass. I really grew tired there of the admiration of the men, and Courtesy of the Women,—I believe they were glad of my departure as I am (you know) too engaging to be known long by sensible Individuals, with Indifference. The last observation would have been more elegant before that which immediately preceeds it, but no matter, we Belle Esprits, love little inaccuracies sometimes if its only with a view to see how our awkward imitators bungle and catch at them. I hate your masculine correctness, its the offspring of dull organs, rather than Genius and good sense, therefore I never affect it.

We have visited five or six settlements since leaving the other Coast. I have endeavoured to make myself popular everywhere; success has attended me and I dare affirm, if it had been the present *ton* to dignify a Conqueress with Laurel that I should have gain'd as many Wreaths as would have formed a pretty rural Arbour. I wish it had been so, for it would have had a good effect & been very refreshing on board a Ship. They all tell me I'm so improved—nothing, I say, to what I was in England: Nobody can contradict the assertion, and if it adds to my consequence you know,—it is good policy. Always self to be the subject of your pen (you'l say) Eliza—why not my dear Cousin? why have I not as great a right to tell you of my perfections as Montaigne had to divulge to the World he loved white Wine better than red? With several other Whims, Capricios, bodily Complaints, infirmities of temper et ct. et ct. of the old Gascoignes, not but I love his Essays better than most modern ones, & I think those that have branded him with the name of Egotist deserve to be Debar'd the pleasure of speaking of or looking at themselves. How is it we love to laugh and yet we do not often approve the person who feeds that voracious passion? Human Nature this! Vile rogue! 'tis a bad picture. However there's a great resemblance. Adieu for the present. 'tis Dark. I will resume my pen tomorrow. I shall be time enough for the Post.

We are now within a fortnights Sail of Bombay. My Husband is second there and in possession of the best Post on the Island, next to the Government. He has purchased a fine House in the Country, where I shall constantly reside. He is always in Town in the Day but sups and sleeps at his Villa. I think we now have a prospect of soon revisiting your Land in Health, peace and Affluence. God grant it may be so. Oh England! thou Country of Liberty! and Climate of good sense! When oh when! shall I hail thy much loved shores! I may be inconstant to my Cousin! I may Laugh and rattle, but believe me I'm serious in saying I taste not of happiness but in the Lap of Content in Britain.

The dispatch of a Sea Post to an English Factory where an Indiaman touches in her way to Europe gives me an opportunity of sending you this, but mention not the receipt of it to our Relations as I write not to them, and it may give offence—once a year is tax enough on a tender Conscience, to sit down premeditatedly to write fibs.

And let it not enter your imagination that you are to correspond with me in such terms as your heart dictates. No my dear Sclater such a conduct, tho' perfectly innocent (and to me worth all the Studied periods of Labour'd Eloquence) would be offensive to my Husband, whose humour, I now am resolved to Study and if possible conform to him, if the most punctilious attention can render me necessary to his happiness, it shall be so. Honour, prudence and the interest of my beloved Children demand the necessary sacrifice and *I will make it*. Opposing his Will, will not do. Let me now try if the conforming to it, in every particular will better my condition.

It is my wish, Sclater, it is my ambition (indeed it is) to be more distinguished as a good Wife than as the agreable Woman, I am in your partial eyes even.—'tis true, I have vanity enough to think I have understanding sufficient to give laws to my Family, but as that cannot be, if providence for wise purposes constituted the Male the Head I will endeavour to act an underpart with grace. " When much is given, much is required." I will think of this proverb & learn humility. Never depriciate Females when many of us can so think so well as your Cousin. A fortnight more I am my own mistress, then Controlled all my life after. Pray for me, that the State may be more pleasing than one of freedom. Indeed my dear Friend I shall ever love you, though I may cease to tell you so E Draper

From ELIZA DRAPER.

From several points of view the letter is interesting. In the first place, its composition clearly indicates the literary influences the writer had recently been under. For example, she speaks of Montaigne with an assumption of profundity of study amusing in its *naïveté*. No one acquainted with Sterne's life and works needs the reminder that he was a profound admirer of the great French essayist, and that many of the novelist's most characteristic plagiarisms were at the expense of this favourite. Addison also shared in the perhaps dubious distinction of Sterne's literary appropriations. A supreme master of style whose writings were greatly in vogue in the middle of the eighteenth century, Addison would most certainly have been cited by the novelist to his fair associate and pupil as the author she should carefully study for the development of her natural talents. Addison's influence is, anyway, distinctly traceable in the foregoing letters. In her deft handling of topics treated and her ironic humour, Eliza catches not unsuccessfully the spirit of the *Spectator* masterpieces.

But it is, of course, the personal aspect of her shipboard correspondence that most concerns the narrative.

In this particular the second communication is exceptionally valuable from the light it throws on the relations existing between Draper and his wife. Manifestly there have been disagreements between the pair, and presumably the breach has been a somewhat wide one, resulting in a display of independence on Eliza's part. But the voyage has given her time to think seriously of her future, and she has sensibly resolved "to study and, if possible, conform to him (her husband)." Honour, prudence, and her children, she says, demand the sacrifice, and she will make it. At the time of writing she could contemplate another fortnight of freedom, but—it must have required an effort to write the sentence—" then controlled all my life after." There is a ring of sincerity in the words in which Eliza conveyed to her favourite cousin her decision to play the part of the submissive wife, and they may be accepted as indicative of the spirit in which she resumed her married life in India.

Early in 1768 Eliza landed in Bombay and settled in the country house " High Meadow," mentioned in the last letter. From this residence some weeks after her arrival she addressed the following letter (No. 7 of Lord Basing's collection) to her aunt, Mrs. Pickering, wife of the Reverend Thomas Pickering, Vicar of St. Sepulchre's, with whom it may be recalled she resided from time to time during her first visit to England :

AS I've a real pleasure in addressing my friends, my dear Aunt cannot Doubt but I very gladly take the opportunity of the Greenwich's departure from hence to England, to convey my best wishes to her.—I flatter myself Dear Madam that the next advices from your land, will give me the agreable Intelligence of your being Easier with respect to health than you was when I left you. England which was ever Dear to me was never so much so as it is now that I'm at a distance from it and have little or no chance of returning to it; for as to looking forward seven or eight Years, its what I never could persuade myself to do, perhaps I'm wrong in not doing it as such a prospect might enable [me] to practise a more severe economy than is usual here, and by such means, an end so desirable might be sooner attain'd, but example is so prevalent and a taste for luxury so predominant that it requires much understanding as well as great firmness, to act in opposition to them. And as I've not enough of the one, and none of the other I must rest satisfied to tread the beaten path and think of passing my best Days in a Country I neither prefer or like.

We had a most agreable Voyage tho' a long one, as it was near ten Months after I left England before we reached this place—but in that time We visited Madrass and several other Settlements which to a roving Genius was truly pleasant. I found my Husband in possession of health and a good Post—providence will I hope continue to him the blessing of the one—and the Directors at home that of the other. My agreable Sister is now a Widow and so much improved in mind and person as to be a very interesting Object. May she be so far conscious of her own work as to avoid throwing herself away a second time. She scarcely remembers you but desires me to present her Duty and best wishes.

The voyage was of such Service to me, as to restore me once more to health & strength. Blessings, I'm now so sensible of, that I shall be very cautious how I endanger them by intemperance or folly; I live intirely in the Country with my dear Louisa, bathe in the Sea daily, drink Milk and have commenced Horsewoman. May you be enabled my worthy Aunt to give me so satisfactory an account of your health as I think myself priveleged to transmit you of mine in consequence of the kind sollicitude you express'd for my Welfare. I say nothing of my Uncle or Cousin Eliza as I mean to write them separately.—Mr. Draper desires his

respectful Compliment and best wishes which Concludes me
Dear Madam your ever gratefully obliged and
Dutiful Niece
BOMBAY, *High Meadow* ELIZA DRAPER.
21st March 1768.
To Mrs. Pickering.

Love of England was still as strong as ever in the writer, but from the tenour of her letter it is clear that the hopes she had earlier entertained of a speedy return home had grown faint. Her reference to the difficulty of economy in the circumstances in which she was placed points to changed conditions in the life of the settlement since her first years there. In actual fact, Bombay in these years was in an active state of transition, due to the increase of trade and the extension of British power in India. In the twenty years prior to Eliza's arrival the population had increased from 70,000 to 140,000. This doubling of the number of the inhabitants had been accompanied by extensive changes in the habits of the European portion of the population. The old simple life almost exclusively lived within the confines of the Fort had been abandoned in favour of a more elaborate scheme of existence. Country houses sprang up in favoured localities some distance away, though Malabar Hill, now the fashionable suburb, was not yet favoured. The Company's senior officials mostly established themselves at Mazagon, the district which to-day is largely given over to commerce, but which in Eliza's time was a salubrious locality clothed with gardens and vineyards and lapped on the harbour side with waters which had not yet been polluted by the contaminations of a vast city.

With the new system of living outside the Fort crept

in a note of ostentation which had been missing in the earlier days. Forbes makes mention of this in his work with a strong expression of regret for departed traditions of simplicity, which is significant of the mischievous influences of the changes. "Etiquette, ostentation, and formality," he said, "had too generally supplanted the urbanity, friendship, and conviviality so delightful in former times."[1]

Forbes is not only a good authority to cite in regard to modes of life: he is also an invaluable witness as to character—Eliza's character. In one part of his work, in alluding to Anjengo and its associations, he speaks of Eliza as "a lady with whom I had the pleasure of being acquainted at Bombay, whose refined taste and elegant accomplishments require no encomiums from my pen."[2] Though a lenient critic Forbes was a severe moralist, and this opinion is of the highest value as the view of a contemporary Anglo-Indian who knew her well and would not have been disposed to gloss over her failings if she were really bad.

When Eliza reached Bombay a change had just taken place in the Governorship. At the time of her departure for England the chief position was in the hands of Charles Crommelin, a member of an old Huguenot family which since his time has been almost continuously represented in the Indian Service. Crommelin was, physically, a fine type of man, and worthily upheld the British tradition. He dispensed a generous hospitality—to the sacrifice of his financial position, which, as his long life closed (he died in 1788 at the age of 81), was little removed from actual penury. An interesting relic of these days which has come down to us is a list of ladies who received invitations to the

[1] *Oriental Memoirs*, vol. ii, p. 380.

[2] *Ibid.*, vol. i, p. 215.

Governor's parties. Eliza's name is seventh on this list, and she no doubt was not the least attractive of the small band of Englishwomen who graced these far-distant assemblages in old Bombay.

When Crommelin's term of office expired early in 1767 the chief position fell to Thomas Hodges, one of the old order of Anglo-Indians to whom "peace and pagodas" was a watchword. The pagodas he already had in great quantity, but peace was hardly his. So uneasily sat his riches upon him that he constantly had at his elbow a seer in the person of a young Brahmin whom he was in the habit of consulting in all the important affairs of his life. This "Hodges' Brahmin," as he came to be known, was a famous character of his day. Forbes has much to say about him in his entertaining pages. The instances he gives of the man's uncanny powers of divination are remarkable. One relates to Hodges's accession to the post of Governor. The appointment was brought about in curious circumstances. There had just previously been an upheaval in the service resulting in Hodges's dismissal from the office of Chief of Surat, which he was then holding, and his suspension from the service. The clouds for him could not have been blacker at the time, as the Court had not only disgraced him but had appointed a colleague and rival, Clive's old antagonist Spencer, to the Governorship. In his perplexity and depression at the untoward course of events Hodges sent for his Brahmin, and upon his arrival communicated to him the events which had lately taken place, concluding by conveying a slight reproach to his seer for having deceived him by false promises of advancement.

The Brahmin with an unaltered countenance coolly replied: "You see this verandah and the apartment to which it leads: Mr. Spencer has reached the portico, but he will not enter the palace. He has set his foot upon the threshold, but he shall not enter into the house! Notwithstanding all appearances to the contrary, you will attain the honours I foretold, and fill the high station to which he has been appointed. A dark cloud is before him!" The singular prophecy was fulfilled to the letter. Very soon after it was uttered an express arrived overland from England annulling Spencer's appointment and investing Hodges with the Government. Naturally the episode created a great stir at the time. Even the cautious Forbes seems to have been carried away by the evidence of the Brahmin's exceptional powers. True, he does not directly admit their genuineness, but he says enough to show that he believed in the man. It was a superstitious age, an age in which witches were still solemnly indicted and sometimes as solemnly burned; an age in which, as we shall see further on in our narrative, trial by ordeal was part of the regular system of British Jurisprudence in Western India.

In the next letter of the series (No. 8 of Lord Basing's collection), Eliza, writing to her cousin Elizabeth, announces the impending termination of her sojourn in Bombay. Her husband had been appointed Chief of the Tellicherry Factory, and thither in four days from the date of the letter—October 28, 1768—she was proceeding with her "family" of thirty, whose care necessitated measures as provident as those of "Noah when he sheltered himself from the Deluge."

THO' I've scarcely time to perform half the business my present situation demands yet cannot I think of leaving Bombay without answering my dear Cousins Epistle, and sincerely did I feel for the loss she must have sustained in our good Uncle, tho I hope it has produced no other bad consequence than what the Death of such a Relation must produce to all his Connections.

We are going to bid adieu to this place My Dear and reside at a Settlement that cannot give us pleasure tho' it may cause contrary sensations in the severest Degree, and this by the Directors Orders. I submit tho' with a very ill grace as the purpose for which we visited India is not answer'd by such a Destination but I'm born to be unfortunate and must bear with what fortitude I can the vicissitudes of misery portion'd out for me; its very difficult for suffering Individuals to say " whatever is—is right " ; at least I cannot till I have gain'd Wisdom which I'll endeavour to acquire in my Exile. if I acquire happiness my Cousin and live so as to deserve it I acquire the best of rewards in attaching a sensible few to my person if not interest and that in good truth I value more than I should the Mines of Peru without friendship and love from some good Beings. You must present my Duty love et. ct. to such of my friends as you particularly style yours, as seriously I've not time to write them.

My departure takes place in four Days ; we have thirty in Family and are necessitated to be as provident as Noah was when he sheltered himself from the effects of the Deluge. I've never heard from your Brother since I left England, which I take extremely ill—and desire you'l tell him so, if you think it will mortify him. Adieu my dear Bess—that Health, Cheerfulness and prosperity may be your constant associates is the sincere wish of your affectionate and obliged

ELIZA DRAPER.

BOMBAY 28*th October* 1768.

From the tone of the letter it is clear that Eliza was not looking forward with any feelings of satisfaction to the new life at Tellicherry. A reference to the records explains the situation. When Hodges was appointed Governor in the remarkable circumstances just related, Draper, though a comparatively junior official, officiated as Senior Member of Council. His signature is appended in this character to the Consultations for

February 2, 1768, about the period of Eliza's arrival. His figuring thus may have been an accident of the moment, due to the absence of senior colleagues on leave, but on the other hand we may detect here the first symptoms of that groundswell of antagonism—or to give it a possibly apter designation, intrigue—which adversely affected Draper's prospects in the period upon which we have now entered. At least it was a decided set-back to be compelled to exchange the dignity and emoluments of the second position in Bombay for the somewhat arid majesty of the Chiefship of Tellicherry.

Not, however, that this was by any means an office devoid of responsibility and of the social prestige which attaches to a high position. With Surat, Tellicherry shared the distinction of affording the most desirable opening for official talent that then offered outside the Presidency. The factory there, founded in 1683, had been throughout the earlier decades of the eighteenth century an important centre of the pepper and cardamom trade of Malabar. Its supervision offered lucrative openings for private trade, paving the way to the accumulation of the fortune to which all high officials aspired as a solatium for years of exile in an unhealthy climate. But those days were past when Draper took up his appointment at Tellicherry.

Chapter VI

At Tellicherry

In the years immediately preceding Draper's transfer from Bombay to the Malabar settlement a great change had been worked in the position of affairs throughout Southern India by the rise to power of Hyder Ali. This redoubtable leader, in 1760–1, attacked and overthrew the ancient Hindoo State of Mysore, and upon the ruins built up a dynasty which, before it had run its course, had shaken the British power in the south to its foundations. After consolidating his position in Mysore, Hyder Ali extended his operations to Calicut, whose prince he defeated in 1766, with the result that a large and fertile territory was added to his dominions. Alarmed at his successes, the Mahrattas and the Nizam of Hyderabad entered into an alliance against him, and a third and unwilling party to the confederacy was the Company, which became involved in consequence of its alliance with the Nizam. Hyder Ali met the menace in characteristic Eastern fashion by making terms with the Mahrattas and the Nizam on the basis of a general alliance against the British.

The deadly peril to the British cause in Southern India thus created was averted by the brilliant military leadership of Colonel Joseph Smith, who was then in charge of the contingent furnished by the Madras Government to its treacherous allies. This body of troops, consisting of only 7000 men and 15 guns, suddenly confronted with a force of 70,000 men and

100 guns, was so cleverly and courageously handled that a complete victory was won, involving the loss by the enemy of sixty of his guns and the greater part of his force.

Important political consequences flowed from this action. Almost immediately the Nizam sued for peace, and as the outcome of the treaty arranged in 1768 the British occupied a portion of the Carnatic Balaghat. Acting on the terms of this compact, Colonel Smith marched from the East into what is now the Salem District of the Madras Presidency, while a force despatched from Bombay to Tellicherry advanced from the West. All went well for a time. While Colonel Smith performed his part of the allotted task with promptitude and efficiency, the Bombay contingent seized Mangalore and Honore after destroying the enemy's fleet. But Hyder Ali was not slow to note that the Western force of the British was a weak one, and he took the field against it with a large army. To avoid an unequal contest which could have only one result the British retreated, leaving their sick and wounded behind them. Hyder Ali thereafter had no difficulty in reoccupying the whole of the Malabar territory he had lost to the British. His army appeared before Tellicherry, much to the alarm of its small garrison. But, believing that the place was much stronger than it was, he refrained from attack. Instead he sought to make an accommodation with the British. His overtures were imprudently rejected by the Madras Government, and as if to emphasize their ineptitude they selected this moment to supersede Colonel Smith in the command of the British forces. They speedily had cause to repent their action. Colonel Smith's successor was an incapable leader who in a few weeks contrived to lose to the enemy all that had previously been won. The Madras Government attempted to retrieve the position by reappointing Colonel Smith to the command of the army. But Hyder Ali in the meantime had strengthened his forces and was now irresistible. In due course he appeared under the very walls of Madras, and there, in April 1769, dictated a peace highly unsatisfactory to the British.

Such were the circumstances in which Draper carried on his work at Tellicherry. He was probably sent there with a view to future developments of the military situation. As the principal seat of the Company's power on the Malabar Coast, the settlement was of exceptional importance from the strategic standpoint. Troops could be readily landed at the port for future operations, and stores accumulated there for their use ; its mere possession was to some extent a check upon the enemy, who always had to be prepared for an attack from this quarter. It was also useful as a convenient halfway house between Bombay and Madras. In many ways it was a charge which could not be safely entrusted to any but experienced hands. How varied were the responsibilities attaching to the position will be gathered from Eliza's letter presently to be given. "I'm by turns the wife of a merchant, soldier and innkeeper," she wrote some time after her arrival. This can be readily understood from the position of Tellicherry as a mercantile settlement on the fringe of the enemy's country and as a port of call for the Company's ships up and down the coast and from Europe. There was a continual coming and going of visitors, involving a heavy drain on Draper's purse in the dispensing of hospitality which was given as a matter of course to all comers.

Tellicherry was a healthy and in many respects attractive station. Eliza plainly liked it. In her letters she several times speaks of it as the Montpelier of India. It deserves all that she says in its favour. Picturesquely situated on a series of thickly wooded low hills stretching away to the seashore, it has a salubrious climate, necessarily hot from its position near the Equator, but with the sultriness of the atmosphere modified by the cooling sea breezes which set in every evening from the west.

A picture of the place as it was in Eliza's day has come down to us in the work of a traveller[1] who visited the Malabar Coast in the latter part of the eighteenth century. The Company's servants then all lived within the walls of the fort, a strongly fortified structure garrisoned by a large number of troops. The residences of the officials were commodious structures, " that of the Chief in particular is not only large but a superb building ; it is situated on the same mount as the adjoining castle, and overlooks and commands the adjacent country and seashore." About a mile to the south, where the dominions of the Company terminated, was another small fort called Mile End, situated so near the northern limit of the French settlement of Mahée "that the sentinels hear each other give the parole." Though the two races were in such neighbourly proximity the British of Eliza's time, as we shall see, had no traffic with " the Monsieurs." The struggle for European ascendancy in India then proceeding to its close was no doubt too deadly for the fraternization of the subjects of the two powers involved.

In the confines of the British settlement were two towns—one occupied by the Portuguese merchants,

[1] *Travels in Asia and Africa*, by the late Abraham Parsons. London, 1808.

" who seem to engross most of the trade," and the other, on the borders of a wood, inhabited by natives of the country. Between the native town and the fort was an extensive open space with, on one side of it, " a pleasant garden belonging to the Chief where the gentlemen of the Factory sometimes pass a little time in walking in the evening." Another garden, more exclusively appropriated to the Chief, " well stocked with flowers," adjoined his residence. These were not the only pleasant amenities of the settlement. In addition there was " a charming shady ride through the wood " where the exiles often took an airing in the evening on horseback or in open chaises, traversing the limits of their little territory from the fort to the southern boundary at Mile End, " near which is an agreeable spot where they usually meet to alight and converse." Nothing is said by Parsons about sport, but in an earlier period the Malabar factories were famous for the facilities they offered for the pursuit of game, in which the adjacent forests abounded. At Carwar, at the end of the seventeenth century, a pack of twenty hounds was kept, and each was allowed two pounds of rice per diem at the Company's expense. In the hunting expeditions the Chief was accompanied by the local Rajahs, and we have a picture of him returning at the close of the day like some Highland laird, accompanied by his native attendants, who, after delivering their compliments with strict formality, part from him at the factory gate.

With Hyder Ali's mercenaries hovering about the outskirts of the settlement there could, in Eliza's day, have been small opportunity for sport. But, on the whole, life ran on agreeable lines with her. She gives a picture of herself in her letters which suggests that the differences with her husband had largely abated, if they had not been entirely removed. In the absence of Draper's clerk and accountant, she acts as his amanuensis, and when she refers to him it is with a note of respect absent from her earlier communications. She must, however, now be allowed to speak for herself. Her first letter (No. 9 of Lord Basing's collection) is a characteristic effusion addressed to her cousin Thomas Limbrey. It opens in the strain of affectionate raillery which she customarily used in addressing her relative. Though there is throughout a suggestion that she is writing with an eye to future publication, she rarely fails to preserve the spirit of a private and intimate communication intended only for the eye of the reader. The letter is long, but it will repay close perusal :

I HAVE at length received an Epistle from my dear Cousin by means of Mr. Purling. Trifles from those we love are ever acceptable, therefore his two written Pages, could not be otherwise, tho' if I'd consulted "*the Bill of Rights*" I should have expected two and twenty, as the Distance between us, the length of our Absence, and the probability of never meeting again, added to the many letters I've wrote him—might I think, have furnish'd more Reflections than his half sheet of Paper contains.

You say, my friend, that you feel Mortified when you're not remembered in my Packet. Now if you, a young Man surrounded with loves, Graces, Pleasure, Health, Wealth, Cheerfulness, and self-approbation, can be subject to Disappointment from the Silence of Distant Friends, judge what I must be, when a Ship from Europe arrives (after passing the year in expectation of such an Event) without any testimony of Remembrance from a Person that Time, Friendship, and a similitude of Temper has long endear'd to me, and whose least title to my regard proceeds [from] his being my near Relation ; the Punctilios of Women may induce me to estimate neglect from your sex, in too serious a light ;

I do indeed consider it, as the highest affront, and think a Renegade Friend deserves as little Compassion, as a Renegade Lover the pride, the Pique of female Dignity, should prevent a union with either! but such Delicacy is I believe, now obsolete, and I'm not so singular as to wish reviving Ancient Virtues, when they interfere with my system of Happiness, which I own to you would be very incompleat without social Connections; and, as the sacrificing your friendship to my Resentment, would be destroying a very considerable link in my Chain, I'm content to continue you in favor, provided I've no more reason to complain, and am convinced that serious affection, rather than the Dictates of Gallantry are your motive for wishing my Correspondence; and you are one of those I'd rather be esteem'd by, than receive the greatest Acts of politeness from, not that my system will allow me to banish that quality from it neither, for I look upon it as very essential in all the Connections of life, more particularly the friendly ones, and cannot but think it betrays a want of policy or delicacy in some well meaning Characters, when they treat their Friends with less good Breeding than they would a common acquaintance; whereas the greatest attention is requisite if they wish to preserve the affection from stagnating; and I verily believe, more amiable sensations have been Destroy'd by the want of it, in Minutiae's than by real or imaginary Deffects in any other particular!

Pray then bear it in your Mind, that I neither can or will pardon neglect a second time, in those I sincerely value! And remember likewise that I am not to be soothed by Athenian Flattery, when it is couched in the Spartan Laconicks! you seem by your letter to suppose the contrary; you are mistaken in my Character, Dear Friend; but for your comfort know, that you're not the first sensible body that has been so; I've a world of Romance in my temper, that I love to indulge because it only leads me to refine upon the best, the sweetest affections of the human heart, not but this passion for the tender Delicate & Elegant, produces some mortifications too, as I seldom meet with persons that come up to my Ideas of perfection, consequently am vastly disgusted *toute en semble* with anything ungenerous,

Illiberal or unfeeling, which I do, & daily must expect to meet with in the common Intercourses of Life.

One of my friends used to tell me, that Art had put me out of my Course, by rendering me the property of Mr. D, for that Nature designed me for an Actress, or the Wife of a very feeling Poet and Philosopher, rather than to a Gentleman of Independance and general Talents, and the reason he was pleased to assign for it was, the natural and supposed qualities of my heart, together with an expressive Countenance, and a manner capable of doing justice to the tender Passions.

I know not whether my friend was right, but I cannot help saying my vanity was gratified by such an opinion, from an acknowledged Judge of Physiognomy and own to you, that I should have more proud pleasure in being considered as the Cibber, or Clairon of the Age than the first Peeress of the Realm, and surely those People betray a want of Understanding that cannot do justice to such Characters! for supposing they preserve a Reputation untainted, who so capable of forming the Mind, or displaying it's Virtues & weaknesses in an amiable and feeling Light? and who so capable of animating Society with those nice Distinctions that give to Beauty, Sense & Cleverness, its principal Charms? For talk not to me of Symmetry & Features, if the eyes are dumb, and every valuable Motion of the Heart cannot be Delineated occasionally from the Countenance by the Pencil of nice Discernment! What sticks of Pens, and greasy sinking Paper![1] excuse my Digressions! shall I apologize for their not being in the Pindaric way? or does it signify whether Pindar or I digress prettiest, so that you're but satisfied? I think not! but I should rather hope you would prefer my Style, because I may write again, and he poor Man! has been Dead long ago.

I know not whether I ought to congratulate you, or be sorry for your near approach to the Wedded State; did I

[1] Eliza doubtless used the native pen constructed from a reed and the coarse paper commonly appropriated to the daily work in the Company's factories. She also probably employed black sand as blotting paper—sprinkling it over the epistle with a vessel like a pepper castor kept for the purpose.

know your Beatrice I should be able to square my Compliments properly but no knowledge whatever, could add to my wishes for your Happiness, as Indeed I think I love you from Principle & Inclination as fondly as ever sister did the best of Brothers. Your Wife will have a treasure in you if she studies your Temper & an easy Companion if not, because I think you incapable of breaking the Peace by recrimination, the exercise of prerogative, reflections ill-natured or illiberal, yes yes—but my Dear Cousin I shall be very apprehensive for you, if she's not an agreable Character in the most Comprehensive sense, because I think too well of you, to suppose you can be moderately happy, notwithstanding all you have urged to me on this Subject; for indeed, my friend there is something more irksome than can be expressed in being frequently subject to an indifferent Object's Society & Conversation and what I'm sure no accidental advantage in the Wealth and prospect way can reconcile a Mind of sensibility to. 'Tis true, your Sex have a thousand means to disengage themselves from Home, but yet they will preserve Appearances if sensible, or Generous, consequently must sacrifice Inclination to policy very frequently, if unhappily connected; and the reflection that they must do so, will poison their most pleasurable Hours, and give a sombre tint to the gayest Manners. I cannot conceive any Society worse than that of Indifferent—'tis worse than miserable! 'tis Contemptible! Milk and Water would be as proper food for a hungry Ploughman, as the Company of a frivolous insensible Woman to a man of observation & Refinement; do not marry what the World calls prudently my dear Coz; if such must be your lot; rather let the Name and Race of your Expectants be annihilated, than commit such Treason to your feelings! I devoutly wish your happiness, but shall despair of it's accomplishment, if your Choice is rather influenced by Interest, than affection; remember I tell you there's no Character under the Sun less qualified to please you than "a good sort of Woman"; it's a Commendation bestowed without Distinction, on Heiresses, Maiden Aunts, Rich Widows, and compositions of "Chalk Water & affection" when no Vices are alledged against them, and no Virtues are visible! 'tis a penance more severe than the Romish Church ever inflicted to bear & be Characterized by the Appellation, when conscious one could attract most wickedly, yet forbear, from motives of real worth—it is indeed of all Denominations, not Vicious, my extremest Dislike! 'tis at best, a sort of don't know as it were, neither this " nor that, nor one, nor t'other, nor good, nor bad; but hanging like Erasmus's Paradise between Heaven and Hell, without vice enough to repent of, or Virtue sufficient to Boast." Were I you, I should say to those who recommended it—" away, away—I'll ha' none on't, I'll ha' none on't."

Perhaps I am rather-selfish in the advice I give, as I own I should not like to see you converted into a Melancholy, *or mere matter of Fact* Man. If it's my Fate to revisit England (which will certainly be the case if Uncles are at all events to be pleased) because then, you most assuredly will see me yawning in your face, as often as I did into that of Mr. Bico's (what's the Mans name? Uncle Joe's Prentice I mean!) when inclination or business led him to speak to me after the tenth hour at Night, and you must not fancy from it that I'm grown proud & indifferent, as such a Nouvelle Conduct from me to you will I assure you, be occasioned by the alteration in yourself! I never could (it's not my talent) support a Conversation for ten Minutes with any Spirit, unless my Companion or Company seem'd willing to advance an equal share of mirth Whim, variety & good humour; this may and I believe is a Defect, but I cannot conquer it, tho' it has led me to be supposed a very silly body, by many *good sort of Women*, and *Matter of Fact Men*.

I am really pleased with your Description of our Worcester Relation,[1] she promised to be a charming Girl when I was there and I sincerely rejoice that she now answers the Idea I then formed of her; Nature I believe has been her only friend for I am sure neither of her guardians were capable of giving Grace to her Motions or assistance to her

[1] Thomas Limbrey Sclater's half-sister Penelope Lutley Sclater, whose acquaintance Eliza had made in England.

understanding ; the pretty Being was quite Savage if not almost an Hottentot when I saw her, and she I hoped, might one day be transplanted from the Field to the Garden, as all beautiful flowers should. She's still young enough to be trained to all the Decorums of good Breeding ; your Metropolis is an excellent School, and I dare say, with her apprehension and sweetness she may one Day make an Interesting figure There ; Pray my love to her, and let her know that I hope to be consider'd as one of her principal Friends when I revisit England.

We are now preparing to leave Tellicherry the Montpelier of India to go to Bombay, D—— is reinstated in his old Post ; it's a profitable one, therefore we have some reason to rejoice. We are all well, and that's as much as I can say. Louisa is much improved in apprehension and manners—but they tell me she's grown proud lately ; I'm sorry for it . . . ? hideous vice, and the bane of good fellowship. I hope to find her as I left her, quite the reverse.

We do not advance in our Fortune ; is not that a pity ? Well but, I should be easy as to that if—ah my friend ! several Ifs are in my way ! one iminently so ! which gives me great perturbation & misery, were you Independent I'd tell you, because I think you love me well enough to estimate my peace at a higher price than a few Hundreds, but—it's in vain to complain—I must bear what results from my own imprudence as well as I can, and yet !—but I'll say no more of it—suffice it to tell you, that I've lived more to my satisfaction this last year than I ever did the preceeding ones ; I am treated with confidence, Destinction & I believe beloved by the Inhabitants of this Place ; I shall leave it with regret from that supposition, exclusive of its having restored me to health, strength & Cheerfulness, I ride on Horseback daily —I bathe in the sea, read Volumes—and fill Reams of Paper with my scribble ; but the Paper, Pens and Ink, are execrable, as this letter will testify ; may the Stationer who provided them be destitute of Sticks and butter all his Life, for reminding me so often of them in the course of this Epistle—and may he if lovesick, be obliged to write to his Mistress on a piece of Glass, without a diamond and with just such a quill as I now wield or rather on a sponge, as that would require more labour.

My Humour might be characterized by one of my favourite sentiments " Mirth without folly, Gravity without Spleen " ; if it were not for the Ifs I mentioned, but they do indeed torture and harrass my mind most grievously, and what's worse, will for these two years to come. Suspense was not made for me—I cannot bear it—would to heaven my fate were decided, or I knew nothing of its being in agitation, but I'm again recurring to this subject, and I shall not know when to leave off, if I pursue it, therefore I'll have done with it after gratifying a Curiosity I may have raised, by acknowledging so far as that two Women, the Widow & Daughter of my best friend have occasioned my distress & Chagrine by threatening to do, what will render me, as the World may think, deservedly unhappy ; their necessities prompt them to the measure, I will endeavour to obviate that Difficulty, but fear I shall not succeed, as what I can do for them is very inadequate to what they may expect from paying no regard to my Sollicitations.—

Pray keep this affair in your own breast my Cousin, as it's addressed to you & you only ; let it then not find another Sanctuary ! excuse my Cautioning you, I have suffered so materially by giving a loose to my pen that I'm likely to repent it as long as I live tho' there's nothing I ever wrote that I could not justify, if I might appeal to Truth & Candour as my Judges ;—but I've been extremely faulty in putting it in any ones power to injure me, by transcribing & communicating what I ought not, the first at the Instigation of one I deemed all Benevolence & truth—the latter to gratify a Curiosity I should not have raised ! If the Event is unhappy as I fear it will be, I must submit with what grace I can ; if not—It will be a warning I'll certainly take !

Adieu, My dear friend, may no perplexities of this or any other sort occasion you ever one painful sensation, on the contrary may you be as happy as health, affluence, & merit can render you !

E. Draper.

Tellicherry 10*th April* 1769.

As a specimen of Eliza's maturer style the letter is exceptionally attractive. There are in it some of the old literary tags which the writer learned from Sterne or perhaps adopted from her favourite authors, but these do not detract from the merit of the communication as a whole. Her lecture to her cousin on the type of wife he should select, with its amusing analysis of "good sort of women" and "matter-of-fact men," is altogether delightful. Towards the end we get a suggestion of the trouble over the Sterne letters which is disturbing her peace of mind. But in the main it is a happy insouciant piece of writing, bubbling over with gaiety.

Chapter VII

At Tellicherry (*continued*)

News of Sterne's death must have reached Eliza very early in her sojourn at Tellicherry. How it affected her we have no means of knowing. Her existing letters supply little material upon which to form an opinion on the point. Others there may have been—indeed, must have been—to Mrs. James and other intimates in which she opened her mind, if not her heart. It is significant, however, that these early months at Tellicherry, when if a passion had really existed on her side Eliza would have been brooding over the death of her lover, were for her a period of exceptional happiness. It would, perhaps, be doing her an injustice to assume that she was relieved to learn of Sterne's death ; but she certainly was not deeply stirred by it. Her chief sentiment associated with the old intimacy was a feeling of anxiety lest the indiscreet traces of it contributed by her hand should be given to the world. How concerned she was we have seen in her letter to her cousin printed in the foregoing chapter. For the folly of giving loose to her pen she was, she said, likely to repent all her life, though there was nothing she had written that she "could not justify."

Not without reason was Eliza thus seriously perturbed for the future. Mrs. Sterne, with the close cooperation of her daughter, Lydia, was intent on making the most of the association of her husband with the wife of the high and presumably wealthy Indian official.

She cared little for the sentimental side of the affair. What she wanted was hard cash, and she was not particular as to how she obtained it. When compromising letters are made the subject of barter the world gives an ugly name to the moral pressure that is applied. But there was a colourable justification for the proposed publication in this case in the fact that Eliza's letters had already been in part made common property by the novelist's action in reading some of them to mixed companies in which he dined. Moreover, Mrs. Sterne's necessities were dire. Her husband had died practically penniless, and with him disappeared the income which a few months previously he had settled on her and her daughter.

A sensitive, high-principled woman, even in these circumstances, would have shrunk from trading in the frailties of her dead husband, but Mrs. Sterne was not of this class. Naturally of coarse fibre, the later events of her life had tended to blunt any of the finer susceptibilities which she possessed. Jealousy of Eliza in the ordinary sense she probably did not feel, but she resented the manner in which Sterne had lavished his money on his friend in the purchase of portraits of her and other costly marks of his affection at a time when she herself was left without what she regarded as adequate means of subsistence. So the papers left behind in the forlorn chambers in Bond Street were ruthlessly exploited to satisfy her pressing needs. In the later correspondence we shall see how the plot thickened. Meanwhile we must allow Eliza to continue the narrative in which in her own peculiar way she gave vent to her feelings and described with many picturesque touches the course of her life.

Her next letter (No. 10 of Lord Basing's collection),

addressed to her cousin Sclater and dated only a month subsequently to the previous one—May 1769—shows her once more as a delightful correspondent. It divides itself naturally into two parts—one in which she deals with personal topics making her cousin a foil for her wit, and the other wherein she sketches graphically and with real force the conditions of life at Tellicherry. As to the personal side of the communication it may be explained that the first uncle mentioned is John Limbrey (1703–1801), owner of the Tangier and Hoddington estates, to which Thomas Limbrey Sclater succeeded. "Uncle Drug" is undoubtedly Joseph Sclater (1715–1769), who carried on the business of Richard Sclater in Newgate Street after the latter's death. Eliza's sister Louisa, married to Colonel Pemble, commanding the troops in Bombay, needs no further introduction.

I HARDLY know what I've wrote, nor have I time to revise correct and so forth, the ship is arrived but only continues in Port for the closing of letters—no person visible from it and whether this will reach you is haphazard.

Its now more than two years since I bid Adieu to England and some dear Individuals that caused my extreme regret in leaving it; not but the Country itself has something very attractive to a person of my disposition and principles, tho' a separation from that alone would never have occasioned more than a few reluctant sighs.—that, time, reflection & Society would soon have dissipated the remembrance of. But to be neglected by those I love (perhaps forgot) truly alarms me. My dear Sclater was one of those friends that render'd Britain Dear to me—and I once thought no time or chance would obliterate the Idea of his Indian Cousin from his Memory if [not] affection, because he seem'd to distinguish her with peculiar regard in the different Periods of Infancy—Youth and Maturity. But what am I now to think? Not one line, my friend, in the seven and twenty long Months that we have been Separated! I well know that absence too frequently terminates the passion of love in your Sex but I hoped that friendship might have been proof against it, as it is a steadier Flame, and requires not such occasional Fuel and self denying assistance as the other. But you've convinced me t'is subject to indifference, if not Caprice for which I forgive you, tho' I shall hardly forget it, while we have each an Existance. Nothing but your absolute Silence (unaccounted for by your sister) could have induced me to believe 'twas possible for you to neglect Mrs. D—— for years. But now! I shall wonder at nothing! except a certain knowledge of Constancy in Men in the articles of Love or friendship, proof against absence, difficulties, time & disappointments! then indeed I might be a happy Model for a Statuary if he wanted one to express the Figure of surprise, and chanced to be near, when conviction had seized me.

This, my friend, is the last letter you will receive from India, till I'm favor'd with one under your own hand, or a certainty of your inability to use the Pen. Till when I shall keep my judgement somewhat suspended tho' it will be a hard task; but our Consanguinity and long united Amity deserve the sacrifice of well grounded resentment. Once therefore I'm content to make it. You see the ties of blood are of some estimation with me, when they coincide with the more agreable ones of affection, tho' I've ever laughed at them and still do. When they are not annexed to the softer Bands of good opinion, kind will, and a diversity of other amiable Qualities, all which I experience for you my dear Sclater, with as feeling a warmth as Delicacy Sentiment and my Notions of friendship can inspire. But I've great pride and so far from wishing to check it, think it my principal Happiness as it enables me to return Scorn with Scorn, and Shun an Intimacy with particular Individuals however distinguished, if they do not meet me halfway; not the first sage in Europe would I bemean [myself] to acquire the notice of, tho he were invested with Power, Beauty and Ermine! a Woman of sentiment may always be a dignified

Being in the Eyes of your sex, if she chooses it—her husband excepted, and to him Tyrant Custom obliges her to be supple—Fame and prudence too dictates it; but o'er others, she reigns! and Triumphantly, unless it be her own fault! You cannot expect, so thinking, so assured, that I should maintain a Correspondence with any Man, when he neglects his part of it, tho' that Man should be yourself. No! my Brother Sclater! or wish to do it either, on the contrary strive to root Out that settled affection in my breast, that has since Girlhood been devoted to you in which I confess that all my acknowledged pride and every justifiable art will be necessary.

We Children of the Sun, never hate or love coolly like some of the Northern Insignificants. Nor do we cover a visit to the Frigid Zone by way of tempering our passions. Away Apathy (another name for Hypocrasy and prudence) keep thy worldly caution and boasted Equilibrium! I wish not a participation of either! The honest African, whose wildness is term'd Savage is far far dearer to me! Why have we an Imagination to conceive, and a Tongue to give our conceptions their due force, unless to be sincere? Prudence! Decorum! forbids! Only so prudence and Decorum are to take the lead of sincerity and honesty! Mighty fine! because we must seem to court the World's approbation whether agreable to us or not. A simple Brahmin would despise such maxims, tho' they're approved in A Scool of politeness regulated by Europaeans.

Upon my word most of your boasted English liberty does not amount to half the freedom the Slaves of Asiatic Slaves experience. Your persons are free, but Minds fettered, the worst and most ignominious destination of Slavery surely. Theirs vice versa; and a widow on the Ganges (the lowest of human reptiles because she's degraded for life and subject to the strikes of a hog feeder) will avow her sentiments more openly (tho' in declamation against the Laws of her Country) than a polish'd Europaean dare so do against the fascination of Custom—and dishonest . . . of Hypocrisy or prudence because dirty interest or some other pitifully . . . makes him dread the ill will of fools in power or a Hydra Multitude, with whom sense and honesty rarely associate.

Were I at liberty to gain a blessing for the distinguished of my friends, it should be the Governing Principles of Asia, with the Mildest Climate of Europe as then Sincerety would be a virtue of the encouraged sort in our beloved Circle, without any regard to the Maxims of those, from whence the Genteel is announced, but " what Charm of instruction can cure the Mind that's tainted " with the love of Hypocrisy under the Specious title of Prudence ? " What Siren voice " awaken the willingly deceived to own that Grimace and politeness, affectation and decorum, are synonimous terms ? And yet my dear Sclater, unless you candidly so think, I may be subject to your censure, rather than praise, or additional tenderness, for declaring I love you more than all my Relations put together (Dear Infants excepted) a thousand & ten thousand times told.

But a truce with my sentimental Observations (Moral and Entertaining) I'll now give you some account of my Situation, Prospects, and so forth—Strange have been the revolutions of Dame Fortune's Wheel to my cost ! since last we hail'd each other. I know you'l pause here to think or say. " the fickle Goddess is seldom Generous, where Nature is kind." thank you, my dear Cousin, for so flattering a Compliment & in return, Ill be very civil and ask you some question of our beloved Sclater, before I enter upon my own Concerns, the first person in " Grammar should always be the last in Rhetoric," this I know, and yet was going to be guilty of a terrible Solecism in good breeding. but I now live out of the World and am encircled with only a few of Natures Simplicities as known to and unknowing refinement, tho' easy good and capricious . . . such a Situation plead my excuse.

Are you married yet, My dear Cousin ? if you are, I will wish you happy and if not that your Wife Elect may have a vast share, not of beauty—thats a foolish thing, but those attractive Graces that are the soul of it ; and may she talk sensibly, dress Elegantly and be as constitutionally good humour'd and vivacious as the Agreable Mrs. D. Have I said too much—have I said too much ? Can you in your heart now deny that I'm a pleasant sprightly sort of Body and " all that " ? I d'ont say I can Cousin, but you should not talk of such things yourself ! and why not my Dear Correcting Monitor, if I'm conscious of deserving them ? Wot ye not that to be vain and know are two things ? did not Montaigne fill volumes with his own Panegyric and Abuse ? and have not I as good Claim to extort due praise, as he had to tell the World he prefer'd white Wine to red ? You must not blame a Woman of my Understanding and Erudition for anything she pleases to do. For in my conscience, I believe, I shall be too hard for you, if you undertake it, as indeed all the sex would for Lords of the Creation ; if like horses we were not ignorant of our own strength. Lady G—— argued justly and well. She was a wise Female and as unlike most of my acquaintances, as ordinary Glass is to a Brilliant.

How go you on with the Tangier Folks ? Uncle . . . has I hear been inoculated. I wish, my dear, if you cannot get them to make you a settlement to your wishes, you would do anything rather than live an inglorious life of Dependance. There's something that sensibly wounds me, in the recollecting Idea of it. Were I Mr. Sclater a pair of Colours, or Rose and Gown would be " altogether preferable ". But this is a Key I'll but lightly touch, as it might produce discord which cannot be in union with your feelings, any more than mine ; and, I wish, none but Harmonious sounds to approach your Ear—and may they ever vibrate, sweet Comfort to your hopes.—

Uncle Drug, I hear is no more, I hope he's in Heaven, there's no harm in that Cousin. I wish all my friends there when they leave us, tho' I would not for Golcondas Mines hasten their departure, what will poor Bess do when my Aunt Pickering is carried off ? She should be heartily welcome to an Assylum with me, if she would accept it, tho' I've no hopes of her fixing advantageously in India ; Sensible and good Girl as she is, as in the first place (forgive me) she's too old. The Men here like some silly Girls in England, like green trash better than wholesome Fruit. Then she's not sufficiently versed in the little Coqueteries to engage the Merchant or seduce the Nabob ; but I shall be glad to see her for all that, and will endeavour to make her life, easy if not happy, if she'll favour me with her Company.

My Sister Louisa is very advantageously Married to the General of our Military Forces after setting all the Amorous Swains in a Flame some Years past, she has closed the Scene well, is deservedly admired (a Charming Belle I assure you), rides in an Ivory Pallenquin inlaid with Gold, and Glitters in Diamonds together with faring supptuously every Day. There's as much difference between her State and Mine, as in the Parabolical rich Man's and beggar's. I'm a mere Lazarus compared to her, but have more Charity than to wish her future lot, like that of Dives's, on the Contrary [I] wish and think she'll be entitled to a place in Abraham's Bosom.—

Mr. D. has lost his beneficial Post at Bombay, and is by order of the Company, now Chief at one of the Factories, Subordinate to it. This was a terrible blow to us at first, but use has in some measure reconciled the Mortifying Change tho' we have no prospect of acquiring such an Independance here as will enable us to Settle in England [for] many—very many Years—as the Country for some has been the Seat of War and still continues subject to frequent alarms from the growing Power of an Ambitious Usurper. I've no doubt, but a General Massacre of the English will ensue, if he once more visits this Coast. Our Fortifications are a wretched burlesque upon such—Troops not better Soldiers, than train'd Bands—and too few in Number, to cope with so able a General and Politician. I was within a hour once of being his Prisoner and cannot say but I thought it a piece of good fortune to escape that honor, tho' he has promised to treat all English Ladies well, that cheerfully submit to the Laws of his Seraglio.

The way of life I'm now in, is quite new to me, but not utterly unpleasant. I'm by turns, the Wife of a Merchant, soldier and Inn-keeper, for in such different capacities is the Chief of Tellicherry destined to act. The war is a bar to Commerce, yet I do a great deal of business in the Mercantile way, as My Husband's Amanuensis; you know his inability to use the Pen; and as he has lost his Clerke and Acomptant without any prospect of acquiring others, I'm necessitated to pass the greatest part of my time in his Office, and content to do so, as it gives me consequence and him pleasure. I really should not be unhappy here if the Motive for which we left England could be as easily accomplished as at Bombay; but that cannot be without an advantageous Peace. Then indeed we should do very well.

The Country is pleasant, and healthy (a Second Montpelier), our house (A Fort and property of the Company) a Magnificent one, furnished too, at our Masters expence and the allowance for supporting it Creditably, what you would term genteely, tho' it does not defray the charge of our Liquors which alone amount to 600 a year; and such a sum, vast as it seems, is not extravagant in our situation, for we are obliged to keep a Public Table, and six Months in the year, have a full house of Shipping Gentry, that resort to us for traffic and Intelligence from all parts of India, China and Asia. Our Society at other times is very confined, as it only consists of a few Factors and two or three Families; and such we cannot expect great intercourse with, on account of the heavy rains and terrible thunder with lightning to which this Coast is peculiarly subject six months in the Year. T'is call'd that of Malabar, and was, before the troubles with Hyder Ally, the source of immense wealth to its principal Inhabitants; the french & Dutch as well as ourselves have each a settlement on it. Mahé is not more than seven Miles distant from us (Yet very few Civilities pass between us & the Monsieurs) & Cochin (a Sweet Spot) about two Day's sail.

The Natives are govern'd by a King, and only subject to our Laws, when within our District; an Inoffensive long hair'd & likely race, they are divided into five distinct casts, and have their Patricians and Plebians as the Romans. The Brahminy is the first, of which their Kings and Priests always are; the Nairs the second of which the Court, great officers and principal Soldiers are composed; then Tivies who bear Arms or serve you as distinguished servants; the Muck-wars only as Fishermen and Porters ; and the Footiers, the lowest of all, are scarcely ever visible and obliged to live in a Distinct Village from the other Casts, where they never stir from unless for Common Necessaries at our Bazar or Market (I shall forget my English), because a Nair or any great Man may with impunity cut them to pieces, if they meet in the same road.

Some very extraordinary Customs prevail in this Malabar Country, such as a King's sisters son succeeding to the Throne in preference to his own children, and it arises from their Indifferent opinion of their Wives Chastity and then the Dignity they say (poor Souls) descends in a right line, for each Monarch is certain whom is his sister, tho' he cannot pretend to discern whether the Queens progeny ought to style him Father. Another (indecent) practise which shocked me amazingly at first—and that is the Men & Women being quite Naked from the Hip upwards, which Savage Custom arose from a Female's attempting to assassinate her Sovereign; the Poynard was conceal'd under her robe in her bosom and in consequence of Detection no Woman has been suffer'd on pain of Death, to have the least covering there since ; a sort of sheet, folded about the Loins with gold Bracelets & Necklaces is the whole of their dress & ornament—both Men & Women.

The Ordeal Trial too, is in use here and I've known Instance of it that would stagger the faith of the greatest Infidel or most [in]credulous. There can be no deception in the affair, as the Accusers have the liberty of preparing the boiling Lead, Oil or red hot bar of Iron ; the accused, in their own Custody, must suffer Death, if the supposed Criminal can put his arm up to the Elbow in the Cauldron of boiling lead (over a Monsterous fire) take a ring, or small piece of Money out, without being the least burnt, or affected at the time, or three Days after. But if the least blister appears he's immediately executed.

I've seen this famous Ceremony—'tis I assure you, a very awful one to the most disinterested Spectator. The accused's Arm is nicely washed and Examined by physical people some Days beforehand; then swathed in many folds of Linnen and made sure by the affix'd seal of the Company, Chief and Accusers after which he's strictly confined till the Day of trial, then unswathed, wash'd and examined again, his Crime read, and affixed to his Waist; a Brahmin exhorts him to confession and reminds him of the immediate consequence of being the least burnt; then the Kindred expostulate and if he knows himself to be guilty, he often forgoes the trial and submits to be tried by a Court of judicature which any Culprit may do. As the above ceremony is never in force but at the request of the accused; the Being I saw undergo it, behaved with the utmost Intrepidity, put his hand into the Cauldron, took out the Coin with vast deliberation & was not the least affected. Then his arm was enclosed in a Bag & bound and seal'd as before; at the Expiration of three Days uncovered and no appearance of blister or Burn; in consequence of which he was acquitted and the Accusers punish'd. This may appear mere Fable, to you my dear Sclater, but it's nevertheless true I assure you upon my honour, tho' I believed it not my self till I'd been an Eye witness of the fact, therefore I shall not be surprized at your incredulity.

The Brahmins are easy, plain, unaffected sons of simple nature—there's a something in their Conversation & Manners, that exceedingly touches me; the Nairs are a proud, Indolent, Cowardly but very handsome people and the Tivies excellent Soldiers in the Field, at Storming or entering a Breach, the latter seems as easy to them, as stepping into a closet. I've acquired some knowledge of their Language and think I'm endued with so much Courage that I should be able to animate them in Person in case of a Siege or Danger. You must not think me vain my dear Cousin, if I tell you I've that happy flexibility about me that easily makes me accomodate myself to a necessary or present situation, and I flatter myself I'm beloved by such of the Malabars as are within reach of my notice. I was born upon their Coast, which is an argument in my favor; then I am neither proud or inaccessible, and they . . . with tokens of affability.

A very clever fellow, that's a Croesus amongst them, is so attached to me, as not to be above the most Menial offices for my Service, and I do not feel the least emotion when he's Daily busying himself in my Bed Chamber with scarcely any more Covering than a gold Bracelet, a mark of distinction bestow'd on him, by his much favor'd Mistress. I move not —out upon the Water—a riding—about the House—but the Creature is my Shadow; and if sickness confines me,— he's twenty times in the Day, by my bed side to make Enquiries or look at me. His terror was excessive when he found I was determined to ride out a horseback without some Gentlemen by way of Escort, and it was, really Dangerous, and what no Woman had ventured to do, before myself. But I never go out without a Guard of six Seepoys (Mahometan Soldiers) arm'd with drawn sabres and loaded Pistols, as some of the Natives are treacherous and might be induced to insult a Woman of *my Consequence* without a Veil.

They have a Custom too of running a *Muck* at a particular season of the year, which is being intoxicated with opium, & then making a merit of slaying every Christian they meet, as the Certain road to Heaven; but this is only the case with the Moplars a discontented race of Moormen, that we are necessitated to tolerate on account of our Commercial affairs. The Malabars are inoffensive enough, our sincere friends and no enemies to our faith (like the Mohometans) tho' all rigid Gentoos.

We are deeply involved in Wars in almost every part of India & with people of the same faith (the Moors) tho' different Interests; how we shall make it out I know not, as Hyder maintains his ground, and we have taught his Troops to be good Soldiers. I very heartily wish myself [back in our] Island before things come to a Crisis, as really the political faces begin to look too apprehensively for our advantage; but I must not breathe such a hope, as now I'm absolutely necessary to Mr. D's business, if not his happiness. But my health suffers in these warm climes, though it is serener than it was at Bombay. Another year and I shall make a grand effort to settle amongst you if I'm not more fortunate here than I have hitherto been. I've not a wish to revisit my last Residence, tho' its the Centre of gaiety, owing partly to Louisa' Marriage with Col. Pemble. To be sure I was almost at the Pinacle of human Grandeur there, but now, "I'm the first of a Village rather than Second of Rome" and should not repine, if Peace and health would befriend my Views.

What an unconscionable letter have I written! Will you greet it kindly, my dear Sclater, or throw it carelessly aside as a Newspaper out of date? Ah! if I thought so! I should be angry indeed! for I cannot bear the supposition of my friendly and fancied effusions being subject to your Contempt. Tho' the hapless Writer may not be possess'd of your former affection, as surely my productions merit some esteem, if it's only in consequence of the sisterly love, I've long been attached to you with.

Adio! Adio! this is or is not, just as you please, the last letter I shall trouble you with, you know the conditions of my correspondence; but I'm wrong, as that cannot be styled a Correspondence where the letters are all proceeding from one side only, any more than that could be stiled a marriage, where the woman importuned the man in vain, to give her a meeting and suffer the Priest to give a sanction to her fondness. Again Adieu! May happiness in the most comprehensive sense be yours! I shall devoutly wish it, tho' I may decline giving you written testimonies of my friendship but till I cease to Exist I think I cannot cease to be your unalterably affectionate in the Mind I am in

E. DRAPER.

TELLICHERRY, *May* 1769.

Exceptional interest attaches to this and, indeed, to the whole series of Tellicherry letters for the insight they give into the life of a factory in Western India in those distant days when Hyder Ali was still a force seriously to be reckoned with by the British in India.

Eliza's contemptuous allusions to the defences of Tellicherry—to the fortifications which were "a wretched burlesque," and to the troops of the garrison "not better than train'd bands," help us to understand the conditions which produced the collapse of British power in Southern India and its sequel, the humiliating treaty of 1768 with Hyder Ali. Tellicherry must have been in imminent peril in this period when "the usurper," as she terms him, was ravaging the country up to the very walls of the settlement. She writes quite calmly of the possibility of a general massacre in the event of a raid, and refers in light terms to her personal danger on one occasion when she was "within an hour of being his (Hyder Ali's) prisoner." The issue of India's future was then trembling in the balance. If at the time the supine Governments of Bombay and Madras alone had been concerned the cause might have been lost for the British. But fortunately there were other and more efficient guardians of the nation's interests in Calcutta who, by their vigorous action in the years immediately following, retrieved the situation.

Eliza's lively account of the Malabar country and its inhabitants brings into prominence the extraordinary racial customs which are found there. The Nairs, who supply one of the most notable examples of a polyandrous race that the world affords, are dealt with by Eliza in her most sprightly vein. She also has something to say about the Malabar custom previously referred to of women appearing in public unclothed from the waist upwards. She explains this practice, which shocked her so amazingly, by stating that it arose out of the attempted assassination of a prince by a woman who had a poniard concealed in her bodice.

In consequence of this episode, she asserts, "no woman has been suffered under pain of death to have the least covering there since." The custom, however, is not so readily to be accounted for. It probably has its sanction in the religion of a remote ancestry of the Southern India people. Certain it is that hundreds of years since the bared breast of a woman was a mark of honour rather than the reverse in parts of the East. In the wonderful paintings on the famous Sigiri rock in Ceylon, which are believed to date to the fifth century after Christ, groups are shown in which apparently royal ladies of a light complexion are being served by dark-skinned female attendants. The former are bare to the waist; the latter are fully clothed. The Buddhistic rock-cut temples of Kenery, in Salsette, show in their carved frescoes the prevalence of a similar practice of fully exposing the bust amongst the regal females there depicted. Other examples of a like kind are to be found in the extensive series of carvings which adorn the remarkable Boro Budur monument of Java, which is believed to be of the later Buddhist period. Religion cuts very deeply into the lives of the people of the East, and the custom plainly indicated as having a sanction in the remote period when these memorials were created may well have lingered in Southern India, where the comparative isolation of the region tended to keep it alive long after it had fallen into desuetude in the northern parts of India.

The account given in the letter of the system of trial by ordeal, which was in vogue at Tellicherry as at other settlements of the Company, is strangely interesting. Eliza's observation that she had known instances of it which "would stagger the faith of the greatest infidel or most (in)credulous" is in harmony with the views of other Anglo-Indian writers of the time. Forbes deals at length with the subject in his fascinating work, giving examples within his own knowledge of its successful working. The most extraordinary of these relates to the detection of a thief who had robbed some of Forbes's valuables and secreted them in a part of his garden. Here the medium employed was not boiling oil or lead into which the accused thrust his arm, but a handful of unboiled rice, which, placed in the mouth and masticated, was regarded by natives as affording a sure test of innocence or guilt. If the accused were innocent the grains, after mastication, were expected to emerge from the mouth a milky liquid ; if he were guilty the product would be a dry powder. At the request of the servants of Forbes's household, all present —including Forbes himself and the suspected thief, a man named Harraby—underwent the ordeal. The result is graphically described in *Oriental Memoirs*.[1] "We were all of the milky party except Harraby," wrote the author ; "mingling with the saliva, it (the rice) became a white fluid : with him it remained a dry powder, notwithstanding a number of fruitless efforts to liquefy it. He was compelled thus to spit it out ; his complexion changed from a rich brown to a livid blue, his lips quivered, and his altered countenance plainly indicated guilt." Eventually he confessed his guilt and received the due meed of his crime. Physiological causes associated with the influence of fear on the salivary secretions are sufficient to account for the phenomenon observed in the case of the accused in this instance ; but the boiling oil test is not so easy to explain. The extraordinary results which attended some of the tests help to an understanding of the

[1] Vol. i, p. 483.

implicit faith reposed in them by the Anglo-Indians of Eliza's time. Occasionally the trial by ordeal or a travesty of it figures in the life of the India of to-day. But it is purely as a native superstition that we meet with it. Modern British judicial procedure scorns such short cuts to justice.

Chapter VIII

At TELLICHERRY (*concluded*)

Eliza's literary output during her sojourn at Tellicherry was more remarkable than that of any period of her life as far as we have records of it. In addition to the two long letters already given there are two others presently to be introduced, and these probably constitute only a portion of her correspondence. She not only wrote copiously: she wrote well, never better than in these years. She seemed to realize that she was living in a critical time, and to feel that her letters should adequately reflect the situation as she saw it from a standpoint of exceptional advantage. Her political reflections, if not deep, are sound. She gives just that detached view of an observer which is often more valuable than the opinion of those whose duty it is to supply the official record of passing events. It is, indeed, not too much to say that these letters of Eliza from Tellicherry are documents of historical value.

The first of the two letters remaining to be noticed before we take leave of Tellicherry has had a rather curious history. From some private collection it passed into the hands of Mr. Edward Daniell, the well-known London bookseller, and was sold by him to Colonel Francis Grant, formerly of the 5th Lancers, who in his turn presented it to the British Museum, where it now reposes with other important documents associated with Eliza. The only indication afforded of the identity of Eliza's correspondent is the reference to a certain Stephen who apparently had been recommended to the good offices of the Drapers. From the general tone and contents of the letter, however, it may almost safely be inferred that Eliza was writing on the occasion to Commodore James. Tom Whitehill, who is referred to in connection with a system of irregular living very general at this time in India, was Eliza's eldest maternal uncle, the son of W. H. Whitehill, mentioned in an earlier chapter. Born about 1721, he was appointed Writer in Bombay in 1741, and was Chief of Anjengo from 1759 until the time of his death ten years later in the circumstances to be related.

MY Dear Sir,—It's with great pleasure I take every opportunity of paying my Duty to you, but more particularly this by the Grenville, as by her I'm enabled to give you a better account of Mr. Drapers Success as a Merchant, than he flatter'd himself with any hopes of, upon his arrival at Tellicherry, and if Fortune continues to be as propitious to us, the six ensuing Seasons, as she's proved the last,—Mr. D—— would not thank the Directors for nominating him to the Government of Bombay. We are both well and entirely contented and wish not to exchange our Situation, but for an Independance in England, which I hope we are in the way of obtaining, and may accomplish in six or seven Years, notwithstanding Hyder Ally Maintains his Ground, and has absolutely refused to listen to terms of Peace from the Madrassers, unless they will make over Trichinopoly to him. this, they think they cannot in point of Honor, or Conscience do—tho' they are heartily tired of the War, & wish to accomodate with him, on reasonable terms—they are now preparing for a long Siege, which he has threatened them with, and if they do not receive Supplies of Money, & Troops, from England, God knows! what will be their fate!—as Hyder is really a very clever, & enterprising Man, accustomed to face, & Conquer Europeans and has for his Secret adviser, one of the best Politicians in India, Governour Laws of Pondicherry.

Whom it is imagined, has always plan'd each of his Campaigns; the Gentlemen of Bengal have drained their Treasury to befriend those of Madrass—but the Governour of Bombay—will not consent to assist them in any respect, tho' he has often been sollicited to do it—and a little timely aid from our Side, might have prevented the present Malancholy prospect, but he says he has no Nosion of Quixotism adventures, and as we cannot benefit by the troubles, he will not risque our suffering any loss,—this argument is very casel, & Superficial, that at first it may appear Specious, tis impolite too, because if the Madrasers are worsted, we certainly shall be the Next Prey—but that, a distant Day, & he always quotes " Sufficient to the Day is the Evil thereof." but he is a poor, despisable Creature, in every respect and as unfit for a Governour—as I am for an Arch-Bishop, not one Individual, is there at Bombay, his friend,—and in short, he never is or deserves to be, Loved, esteem'd, or feared.

We are very particularly interested in Hyders success, at this Settlement, as he has most of the Country powers about us, in total Subjection, & infests our Coast, with his Fleet, to intercept our Merchantmen, their's no leaving us, now for Bombay, with any Safety without a Convoy & the Bombay Cruisers, three or four of them, are Stationed between Carwar, Onore & Mount Dilly for that purpose. We are terribly infested too, by the Cooley Boats & Mollawans. the Morattas, had the Insolence to surround Bombay with their Fleet a few Months since, which did not a little terrify our Pusillanimous General, but they soon dispersed when the Commodore received Permission to ask them some questions, its imagined this Bravado was effected at the Instigation of Hyder, to Divert us from all thoughts of sending Troops to Madras, it answer'd his hopes—but if he had bribed the Governours Brahmin to be his friend, it would have done as well, for nothing in Public, or domestic Concerns, is transacted at Bombay, without that Fellows knowledge & consent. Some of the Gentlemen by way of reprimand, have advised Mr. Hodges to give him a Seat at Council. Our Island is now very Populous—very expensive, very improvable, & would be very flourishing, if we had a proper Man at the head of affairs.

This Coast has been vastly injured by Hyders Ravages, 'tis nothing in Comparison to what it was some Years ago, but would still be the Source of profit to the Company, & a Tellicherry Chief if the War was once happily terminated. —Most of the Gentlemen that distinguished themselves, by behaving ill at Mangalore, have been broke by a General Court Martial at Bombay, it was a tedious affair—lasting upwards of six Weeks, tho' the Members Met Daily,—

This My dear Sir, is all the Public Intelligence, I can recollect worthy of transmitting you, and now for a little private, Tom Whitehill, my kind Uncle, is well—I often hear from him & he must by all accounts, have made himself independant by this time. he is increasing his Family of Natural Children, but declared to me, that he never would give them more than five thousand rupees each, because he would not tempt any Gentleman to Marry them for the sake of Money, and he had rather dispose of them to Phesendars of their own Colour—than to Europeans—he has one Daughter Marriageable, two Young ones, & two or three infant Sons.—I never hear from Jack Whitehill, but I know he is well from my Correspondents at Madrass, I hope he does not maintain a Silence to his English friends, as . . . should be a good Accomptant & write swiftly. Mr. Draper would be very glad of him here—make it worth his while, and keep him out of harms way, as he is in want of just such a Person, You know his inability to use the Pen—he has lost his two Clerks too, & if I was not capable of assisting, & maintaining his Correspondence for him I know not what he would do at this juncture. I only fulfil my Duty—and have not the least Merit in it as a good Purvoe that thoroughly understood English and spelled properly—would answer his Views still better.

Louisa is very advantageously Married, to the Commander of our Forces, a Colonel Pemble, he is handsome, amiable, and Magnificent in his temper—his Income amounts to thirty thousand Rupees a year—but I fear they stand little chance of saving a Fortune, as they are Gay—extravagant & fond of Company, but I know not if it signifies much—as they love India—are healthy, admired, and esteemed here and not very desirous of exchanging affluence in the Eastern . . . fondness and is a Prince in Spirit and occasional good works. they are on no terms with the Governour, neither visiting or being visited by him.

A Mr. Banister, that is much older than yourself & formerly knew you in the Service, now resides here—he desired me to present his kindest remembrances to you, assuring you of his Unalterable esteem & good wishes. The good Man & his Wife live very comfortably—are well, and much noticed with respectful attention.

I hope to be favor'd with long & interesting letters from Europe by the next Ship—England ! which was always dear to me—was never so much so as now !—the Welfare of my dear Children, sits very near my heart, & I cannot help feeling great anxiety on their account, tho' I am confident of Mrs. Whitehills care and best attention to their true Interest, God preserve the poor babes ! may they live to give satisfaction to their Parents—and reflect honour on their amiable Protectress ! I hope you had an agreable Summer in the Society of my friend and little . . . by presenting my Compliments to him, and best wishes for his health and enjoyment of England, we now wish him our Head again, would to Heaven he had not left us a Prey to the foolish policy and for Cunning of an Hodges ! the wish is entirely general. Not a Moist Eye or grave Countenance will be visible on his Departure, unless it's his Female Cuffary Shirt airers, for a few Rupees, or mere form's sake, oh ! he is gloriously hated ! and I prognosticate, ever will be so—even by the Wife of his Bosom—if he is Dotard enough with his jealous propensities and Selfish particularities, to make a Second choice ! but no,—his avarice will prevent his Marrying again, for a good Woman would loathe his Wealth with such an Incumbrance as himself—and a bad one . . . happy—prays your ever grateful and . . . Child

ELIZA DRAPER.

TELLICHERRY *April* 1769.

P.S. Mr. Draper presents you his respectful Compliments with . . . assurances of his doing every thing in his power for Stephen, if you (send him) to Bombay.

Though the writer travels over much the same ground in this as in her two earlier letters, she yet contrives to impart a freshness to her subjects. Her versatility is especially shown in describing the military position as it was left at this juncture by the disastrous retreat from Mangalore. A vigorous sketch is given of the dangers threatened to the British power by Hyder Ali's successes, coupled with an attack on the Bombay Government—and particularly its head-Governor, Hodges—for the inadequate support they had rendered in the crisis. We get here an echo of controversies which convulsed Western India in the mid-eighteenth century period and lingered long afterwards.

Mangalore was the central point of this political and military storm. The port is now merely a pleasant Malabar coast town, best known for its manufacture of a very excellent kind of roofing tile. But in Eliza's day it had exceptional importance as one of the best strategically placed ports of the western coast. Hyder Ali early recognized its value and established at it in 1763 a dockyard and arsenal. The capture of the port and its subsequent recovery by Hyder Ali have already been mentioned, but this does not complete its chequered history. In 1781 the British were again in occupation, only, however, to be evicted three years later by Tippoo Sultan, Hyder Ali's successor, after a gallant resistance. Finally, when that prince was decisively defeated and killed at Seringapatam in 1799, Mangalore became British territory and has remained so ever since.

The Mangalore court-martial was the device which the Bombay Government adopted to divert attention from their own laches. The broken officers in some cases deserved all they got in the way of punishment, but they were hardly the less scapegoats on that account. Who the real culprit was in the view of Tellicherry people Eliza is at pains to indicate. In all her letters there is nothing more scathing than her attack on Hodges. The very bitterness of it suggests the existence of a grievance—one probably associated with Draper's transfer from Bombay. But Hodges was certainly not an estimable character either in his private or public relations. He had at this time amassed a great fortune by methods which, if not actually dishonourable, were of questionable propriety. Unmarried, and with no apparent family ties, he had become what Sir James Mackintosh afterwards called " Brahminized." His strange partiality for Indian ways was most conspicuously shown in connection with the Brahmin friendship already alluded to. The Hindoo seer and he became more inseparable as time went by. A strange Bombay legend even associated them in death. The story, as related by Mr. Douglas in *Bombay and Western India*, is that the Brahmin predicted that the night of February 22, 1771, would be dangerous to the Governor, and that the next morning Hodges was found sitting up in bed with his forefinger on his lips, as if enjoining silence, stark dead.

A noteworthy change in the Drapers' circumstances is recorded in the early part of the communication. We hear no more of the difficulties of making both ends meet. On the contrary, Draper had done so well that if the next six seasons were as good he would not thank the directors for nominating him Governor of Bombay. There is nothing to explain the reason for the improvement in prospects referred to in these striking terms. But it was probably due to the easing of the military situation, which allowed goods previously kept back to come to the coast. As the then principal calling place on the Malabar Coast for ships from home and from the eastward, Tellicherry was, in normal times, a considerable mart. Apart from pepper, the staple product, a brisk trade was done in areca nuts, ginger, cocoanuts, cocoanut oil, coir ropes and yarn, and cotton cloth. The cotton manufactures were exceptionally cheap and good. A local speciality was a particular kind of towel which, Parsons says, was esteemed the best in India.[1] Under the Company's regulations it would have been open to Draper to conduct quite an extensive private trade. Even at that period Anjengo, though much decayed, was said to be worth to the holder of the Chiefship £3000 a year. Probably the Tellicherry appointment held much greater possibilities in the favourable circumstances sketched.

The last of the Tellicherry letters (No. 11 of Lord Basing's collection) is mainly of domestic interest. Dated October 27, 1769, it is addressed to the writer's cousin Elizabeth, in reply to a letter from her announcing the death of her aunt Pickering, to whom Eliza was so warmly attached. The grandfather mentioned in the letter is, of course, Charles Whitehill, of Worfield, in Shropshire, with whom Eliza left her two children, the elder of whom had just died in his tenth year. The "Uncle in this neighbourhood" is Thomas Whitehill, above referred to.

MY dear Cousin,—I was greatly pleased with the Receipt of your Letter by the *Campden*, tho' it contained a piece of Melancholy Intelligence I was prepared for, by an Epistle prior to yours, from my Grandfather. the very bad State, our good Aunt so long labour'd

[1] *A Voyage to India*, p. 237.

under, must enable us to think her Death an happy event for herself, especially as her Moral & religious Principles, added to the whole tenor of her actions gives us reason to believe her afflictions ceased, with her Existence, and that she is now a far happier Being than any Worldly attention could have rendered her. but 'tis Natural to lament the Decease of a Friend from selfish motives, & perhaps 'tis more laudable than otherwise that we should do so, because some of the best affections of the heart are exercised by it; but I shall get out of my depth if I moralize any further, and you may suppose I'm giving you the Tag of an old Sermon whereas you deserve the first fruits of the Church rather than it's leavings.—

I received the ring you obligingly enclosed for me, and highly approve the addition you made to it, I have it now on my finger—and it but too well corresponds with my dress, the Mournfulness of which is occasioned by the Death of our poor little Boy and that of an Uncle in this Neighbourhood.

Had it suited you to visit India my dear Bess, I think I could have answer'd for your Situation being as pleasant, as Friendship Cheerfulness & good humour could have made it. I am neither powerful, or rich, but I've a heart, my good Girl, that naturally expands when worthy objects present themselves to my View or Memory, and that advantage, together with a few & cts would I think, have endeared me to you; but you're right in not coming amongst us, and I love you the better in remaining satisfied where you are from such grateful & sensible Motives as you Assign. Pray give my Duty to my Uncle & assure him I do not wish or mean that he should tax himself to acknowledge my Epistles. I naturally enquire after all my Connections from a principle of kindness, and if I receive satisfactory replies, it imports very little what channel they come thro; I sincerely hope he's mistaken in his own case, with regard to being Superannuated and that he supposes the symptoms of declining Bodily Strength those of the Mental Faculties, which I long wish him the entire possession of, from a persuasion that a Good Mans Influence is very important to Society and cannot be too extensive & durable.

I have lately, for the first time, received a Letter from your Brother ; had any person told me, he could have neglected your Indian Cousin so long, I should have despised 'em as false Prophets, & wonder'd how they came to suspect me of such weak credulity, as to think I'd rest my faith on improbabilities ; you may tell him to prepare for a scolding Letter, which he will certainly receive, unless I change my mind, a thing not impossible, as I pretend not to the gift of Consistency, when such variable Objects as Anger ill humour & young Men occupy my attention.

We are now preparing to leave Tellicherry for Bombay a circumstance that would not delight me, if I did not hope for a greater share of " Peace & Pagodas " there than here, had I visited the East with an Intention to fix here, this Place had suited me better than any I have seen. I'm the Queen of it ; but not so far of Ceasors Mind, as to think the first station in a Village preferable to the second in Rome ; my ambition extends no further, than being the ninety ninth Character in England, in point of Female excellence, Wealth & two or three acres ;—there's humility for you ! My Sister is well, amiable, encreasing her Family, and so forth. Adieu my dear Bess ! pray remember me to such as I know & Love of your acquaintance ! I wish you a good Portion of this Life's best Things & am with sincerity & affection your Devoted

Tellicherry 27*th October* 1769. Eliza Draper.

P.S. Mr. Draper presents his sincere Regards to my Uncle yourself & Family.

Be it known unto you, that we are subject to Wars here and that Pagodas are a Gold Coin of the Country. Peace & Pagodas to you.

For the first time we hear of Draper's impending transfer from Tellicherry. Eliza evidently contemplates the prospect with regret. She repeats to her cousin an expression she has previously used when she says that she was "Queen" at Tellicherry. Then wistfully her thoughts turn homewards. She would not subscribe to Cæsar's view that the first station in a village was preferable to the second in Rome; her ambition went "no further than being the ninety-ninth character in England, in point of female excellence, wealth, and two or three acres." Eliza's final wish of "peace and pagodas" for her cousin embodies a familiar Anglo-Indian sentiment of early Indian days. It had been long in currency, even when Eliza used it. Thus, Sir John Gayer, Governor of Bombay, in a communication to the directors from Bombay Castle under date June 30, 1699, writes of a colleague on his Council: "Mr. Colt is no ill-designing man . . . but then he is for peace and pagodas and not able to stand a brunt when any trouble appears."[1] Eliza herself was ardently for peace and pagodas, but, unhappily, neither peace nor pagodas was for her. Soon after writing the above letter she entered upon the most distressing period of her life. But before that phase was reached she was to share with her husband another spell of isolated majesty as "Queen" of the little community of exiles at Surat, whither, after a short stay in Bombay, her husband proceeded on quitting his post at Tellicherry.

[1] *Indian Records, O. C.*, vol. lv.

Chapter IX

At Surat

In exchanging Tellicherry for Surat the Drapers entered upon a famous commercial and political sphere. Though its glory had faded since the days of Mogul ascendancy, though its once arrogant Governor, before whom all Europeans humbled themselves, was now a puppet in British hands, and though the Great Anarchy had circumscribed the city and devastated its outskirts, it was still a centre in which Oriental magnificence found vivid expression. In its crowded streets traders from every part of the East and from most parts of Europe jostled each other, and its palaces, though outwardly dilapidated and even mean in appearance, within gave evidence in their marble seraglios and their scented fountains of the persistence of luxury even amid the ruins of Mogul power. The beautiful gardens, too, for which Surat was famous in the seventeenth century, still offered to the eye that riotous mass of colour and to the sense of smell that overpowering odour which so impressed the early European visitors to the port.

Perhaps because of the decay of the native authority the European factories, British, French, Dutch, and Portuguese, maintained something more than their old magnificence. The outgoings and incomings of their chief functionaries were marked with the pomp of almost royal state. When they paid their formal visits they were received with the deference reserved for the great. Especially were these the conditions under which the leading British representative discharged his duties.[1] He was in a very real sense the power behind the throne, and while he acted up to the part the world at large were not slow to pay him suitable homage.

The "Queen" of the British settlement of Tellicherry thus by the transfer became the monarch of an ampler and more dignified kingdom. If display pleased Eliza, as certainly it did, she could not fail to find everything here to her heart's desire. Her palankeen, when it went out, would be attended by running footmen, who would clear a way for her dainty form by methods of coercion which would shock a modern democrat. If she elected to drive, an escort of horse would guard her coach. Even if she ventured in the cool of the evening to walk in the delightful Company's garden on the outskirts of the city a host of satellites would follow in her train. Happiness would have been hers if happiness had been possible, but alas! she had passed beyond the stage when the externals of her conditions in India were of avail to influence the drift of her mind, which was more and more definitely tending towards a crisis in her marital relations. There is only one letter written from Surat known to exist (No. 12 of Lord Basing's collection). Written on April 5, 1771, it is addressed to Thomas Limbrey Sclater, the favoured recipient of so much of her correspondence.

[1] "When the English Chief goes out or comes in at the gates the drums beat and the guard is turned out; which ceremony is observed when he passes the main guard, which is on the Esplanade near the Castle: besides two union flags borne before his carriage, it is preceded by a sergeant and twenty sepoys with swords drawn, who run before it from the gate to his house, where the guard is turned out on his arrival and drums beat."—Parsons, p. 252.

There is an undercurrent of dissatisfaction and discontent in it which is impressive.

I FORGET my dear Sclater whether I wrote you by the last Ship or not. I never keep or make Copies and therefore am not so certain about the writing Business as in policy I could wish to be. Memory not having blessed me with her retentive Power in any degree equal to my Wishes; I received your affectionate letter my Dear Coz—and I prophecy that I shall answer it very stupidly for I danced last night, supped on a cool Terrasse and sat up till three o'clock this morning; this may appear nothing very extraordinary to you, my spirits and love of the graceful Movement considered, but it was a very great undertaking, the Climate, my Plan of temperance & exercise consider'd. For you must know, that I find it necessary to live simply Mechanical, in order to preserve the remains of a broken Constitution and some traces of my former appearance—I rise with the Lark daily—and as constantly amble some eight or ten Miles—after the Fox too, occasionally.

Our Field Sports have something Royal with 'em here—what think you of Hunting the Antelope with Leopards? This I have frequently done—and a noble Diversion it is.—Early Hours, and an abstemious Diet, are absolutely necessary to the preservation of Health in India and I generally conform to the one & invariably practise the other; ten or eleven o'clock at the latest, is the usuall time of retiring, and soup and Vegetables, with sherbet and milk constitutes the whole of my Regimen, still I cannot acquire anything like confirmed Health or Strength Here—but if this mode of living preserves my Being, my Cheerfulness and natural disposition to make the best of things, will I hope teach me to bear it,—and with a tolerable degree of relish too—for I will studiously have recourse to all my Powers, to second this Care, and that time and Chance befriending me, I shall live to share some of my best Hours with you, my Cousin, and a few others that are dear to me in your Land.

At least I will not thro' any fault of my own, return to Europe with the Dregs of Life only but endeavour by every honest means to preserve such a portion of animating spirit, as may qualify me, for the Character of an agreable Companion—and then, who knows, but Cool Weather, fashionable Society, and the Animating Presence of those I love may enable me " formed by their converse, happily to steer, from grave to gay, from lively to severe," for I have in my Nature, such propensity " to catch the living Manners as they rise." I say not this from any principle of vanity, as indeed I think it argues no more Merit in myself than if I had said I could fly, supposing I really could do so, from Heaven having been pleased to affix a pair of Wings to my shoulders. Do you know that I begin to think " all praise foreign but that of true Desert." It was not always so, but this same solitude produces reflection, and reflection in good minds is an enemy to every thing that is not founded on Truth—consequently I grow fond of my own approbation and endeavour to deserve it by such a mode of thinking & acting, as may enable me to acquire it.

Seriously my dear Sclater—I believe I shall one Day be a good Moralist, and, I think, I should be a good Member of society too, if my Power was equal to my benevolence & desire of extending liberality to all worthy sufferers in Distress—at least, this, I am sure of—that I have not an Idea, of any Worldly happiness interesting my affections, so much, as the system laid down & observed by my favorite Character—Popes Man of Ross—His Plan I think and hope would be mine ; and I am sure that I've enthusiasm enough in my Nature, to undertake a Pilgrimage from hence to his Tomb—merely for the sake of contemplating the spot—sacred to the Memory of such Philosophy ! And yet those that know me, think not thus of me ;—My character in the eyes of Worldly Wise Ones—is at best nothing more than that of a gay dissipated agreable Woman—but I ought not to be offended at this opinion entertained of me, as I think nothing more of the best of my associates, whose title to praise might be superior to mine, if they had opportunity of manifesting their sentiments by practical Humanity, and our Actions were to be fairly stated in Reason's Balance ;—for the men here are generous enough in their prodigal way—and who knows but this same principle, properly directed, might lead them to be silent dispensers of Bounty in a climate where Ostentation was not classed among the brilliant Qualities.—

As to the Women, they are in General, a set of Ignoramus's, or at best pretty Triflers—and I do not covet their society much from my dislike of hearing the subjects of scandal & dress perpetually canvass'd, and such are the only Topicks, that enliven a female assembly in India. But this same dislike, added to a frankness that is natural to me, in the Society of conversible men—subjects me to very mortifying Insinuations, and disagreable difficulties in the petty way—as I cannot counteract my Nature, so far as to feign a liking or Complaisance for the Company of my own Sex only,—and they have just observation and address enough to give a malicious turn to my Conduct, tho' incapable of distinguishing the motive for it :—this is but too natural an Infirmity, to the *half* deserving and ever will remain so, while self Love makes us blind to our own defects.—it is only the amiable and good that will attempt to justify a preference given against themselves & cheerfully award it of their own accord, from a natural disposition to state every thing in the kindest manner, while any one action will admit of more than one Inference.

India, my dear Cousin, is I believe, the very last Country, that an agreable Woman should expect to live uncensured in —and yet, I think, it abounds with fewer temptations to frailty, than any I have yet seen—but such is the mode of thinking and Acting in it—that it is everything but impossible, for an ingenuous minded Female of tolerable appearance—to pass unsuspected or unreproached here. This chiefly arises from the want of Judgement and kind Consideration in its Inhabitants—for tho' the Access to familiarity, is very easy while nothing more is meant than Trifling —Conversation—or real Friendship, yet nothing can be more difficult than the Management of illicit attachments ; from the peculiarity of our settled Economy, as to Houses, Servants, and a long &cts and none, I am confident, but Women of extreme Clever Heads—or very abandoned Principles, could think of accomplishing so difficult a Purpose.—We abound not, with the one or the other, and those that are best amongst us—have a sense of reputation that counteracts the partiality in favour of a foreign Object; and the Danger alone—is sufficient to deter the silly minded,—consequently I take it for granted—that out of a hundred Women that are aspersed—not more than one of the Number, is in reallity deserving of it—this Calculation is more than possible, t'is highly probable—as the difficulties in the road to Intrigue are so various and alarming—that I verily believe they never occur to minds of any worth, without operating as an Antidote to Passion—therefore pray think generously of us Indian fair ones—and be our Advocate when you hear us traduced (which you often may) as a set of Ignorants, unknowing in every thing, but the Rites of Venus.—

I am glad to hear that our Uncle is prefer'd, if it will benefit his situation and our Bet's prospects in any Measure; if not—who will, may wear Mitres for what I care—for as to the Honor of the thing—I'd rather receive a billet from my dear Sclater—subscribed my affectionate coz—than a whole Paragraph from the right Reverend Himself setting forth, *as how, that he was* invested with the Pontefical ornaments of such a See—on such a day—and was thought to make a goodly *Apostolic Appearance* therein—for I scruple not to think and say, my dear Friend, that all my kinsfolk are in comparison of Thee, as trifling in my Estimation as my little finger is in Comparison to my two bright Eyes—and so, without the Gift of Prophesy I could foretell—that they ever would remain.—

You are not Married yet I find—I wish you were, and to a deserving Being—as then I should hope to pass some of my best Hours with you, when I revisited England;—the World will not let us be much together, without scandalizing us—if you remain single—tho' we are near relations, and perhaps love each other better than the generality of Brothers and Sisters do—but your Wedlock State, would settle everything, if your Wife liked me and if she did not—why I must submit, & exclude you my social Compact—tho' I never should banish your brotherly seat in my affections—

What do you allude to by talking of public Measures? are you aiming at a seat in the House of Senators? I wish you success in all your schemes—and wish you happiness too—tho' that does not always attend the accomplishment of our best Projects—I must, I fear, be content to wear out my bloom, and patience in this languid climate and stupid Society, for I see no prospect of gaining Health or Riches—but by such Means, as are worse than the Diseases of a Valetudinarian State—and simple Poverty.—Gods will be done! I would endeavour to obviate so Melancholy a situation, by every effort in my Power—but if it is not to be done—I would submit with a Grace—and live in Hopes, that some unforseen Chance, of the kind sort—might do that for me, which human foresight could not accomplish.

Purling is now in the Chair and if his Interest with the Directors is equal to his Inclination of serving us, I flatter myself he will do something considerable for us. He is an amiable good tempered Man—and always professed an affectionate Regard for your Cousin which authorizes me to think, he will not be unmindful of our Interest—the D—I never intended a severer Punishment, than that of a dependent Situation, for one of a free generous Spirit—it curbs every valuable Emotion of the Soul, and debases the Dignity of the mind, by obliging it to pursue a course of action, only natural to the Illiberal & Illiterate!—Oh! that I had a thatched Palace & decent Income of my own! then would I read what books and see what Friends I pleased & Maintain an Independents Dignity & Ease too! You'l think that I'm grown pedantic, & immensely fond of Quotations lately—no matter, so that you do, but do me justice, in other points—one of which, my affection for you will not suffer me to dispense with, and that is, believing me, your unalterably faithful & kind Friend

E. Draper.

Surat *5th April*—my birthday 27 to Day 1771.

"My birthday, 27 to-day"—Eliza reminds her cousin, and the statement supplies the only exact record we have to fix the day of her birth. It is well that the reader should not overlook the entry. The girl-wife is still little more than a girl. In ordinary happy circumstances with her twenty-seven years only behind her she would be but on the threshold of domestic life. How different are Eliza's conditions! She is outwardly lively, she dances until three in the morning, she is up with the lark every day and occasionally hunts the fox. But her heart is more and more hardening towards the union into which fate has thrown her ; more and more she is overwhelmed with homesickness and with a desire to flee from " this languid climate and stupid society." That is a significant passage in which she dwells on the difficulties and dangers which attend intrigues in India. The defence she there puts forward for the supposedly erring sister seems to be an echo of what she might have written later.

As a picture of the life of an Englishwoman at Surat in the middle of the eighteenth century Eliza's letter is not excelled by anything extant. The whole scene is brought to view in the vigorous sentences in which she describes her occupations. The allusion to the hunting of antelopes with leopards shows her keenly appreciative of a form of Guzerat sport, as novel as it is exciting. In modern times the opportunities of seeing this sport are confined to Native States like Baroda, where the Royal Cheeta Hunt is as distinctly a part of the regal system as the Royal Buckhounds is, or was, of our Royal Household. There, if the visitor is so fortunate as to have an invitation on a great ceremonial occasion, he will join at early morning in one of these thrilling hunts. The cheeta, secured by a string or chain, and with a belt round his loins, is taken out in charge of a keeper in a bullock-drawn cart. When a likely place for the discovery of game is reached, a halt is called and the cheeta is held in instant readiness for pursuit if deer are viewed. Soon this happens and the cheeta is released by his keeper. The animal drops quickly off the cart and creeps forward with the greatest cunning until it reaches a favoured point about seventy yards from the prey, when it rushes forward with extraordinary speed, ultimately in most cases overhauling the deer, upon whose neck it fastens with deadly intent.

Forbes in his work[1] gives a spirited description of cheeta hunting as he saw it, in almost exactly the same year as that in which Eliza participated in it. Here it is stated that when the cheeta resolves to exert himself "his velocity is astonishing; for although the antelope is esteemed the swiftest species of the deer, . . . yet the game is usually caught." The writer describes vividly the kill: "The cheeta, on overtaking the deer, by a most powerful and dexterous use of its paw overthrows it, and in the same instant seizes it by the throat, when, if it is young or a doe, it does not quit its hold until he finds the respiration cease; but if it is a buck, whose neck is very thick and powerful, he is obliged to be more cautious, and to avoid in the struggle not only a blow from the horns—which, from the convulsive motion of mere terror and agony, might be very dangerous—but from the hoofs, whose sharpness renders them equally so; the artful care with which he avoids these weapons is truly astonishing. The deer thus seized by the throat loses all capacity of struggling, and in the interim the cheeta keeper comes up and instantly cuts the throat of the antelope. . . . The cheeta, finding the animal dead, would commence the work of laceration, . . . but is prevented by his

[1] *Oriental Memoirs*, vol. i, p. 173.

keeper, who either catches the blood from his throat in a ladle kept for that purpose, and presents it to him to lap, or nimbly cuts off the last joint of the leg, and putting it into his mouth he leaves him employed with it and quickly carries off the game to secure it behind the hackery (cart). The cheeta having amused himself with his ladle or bone, his keeper leads him to the cart, which he ascends without taking any further notice of the game, though tied close under his nose." Such was this truly royal sport in Eliza's day, and such it is to-day, though the conditions now are not so favourable as they were in the eighteenth century when Guzerat was much more thinly populated and less cultivated than it is at the present time.

Chapter X

At BOMBAY—*on the* EDGE *of the* PRECIPICE

Early in 1772 another change in Draper's circumstances brought him back to Bombay to his seat on the Council there. He lost his "lucrative post" at Surat by neglect of the orders of Government, combined with what was regarded as his undue interference with the Military Commandant. We may hazard a suspicion that other more subtle causes were at the root of his disgrace. The Indian service of that day was honeycombed with intrigue, and Draper was just the type of man to excite the hostility, open and secret, of his colleagues. In this instance he seems to have had a distinct grievance. Eliza, in referring to the subject, as will be seen presently, comments upon it with a note of indignation which hardly would have been sounded had her husband been less directly a victim of an unfair rivalry.

However strong her sentiments on this point may have been, Eliza was becoming daily more estranged from her husband. No open breach occurred—not for lack of material for a separation, but simply because neither party as yet desired it. Draper, as a leading official, had the conventions to restrain him. Moreover, he had no desire to part with so attractive a head of his domestic establishment as his wife was, even though the ties between them had now worn to the utmost point of attenuation consistent with continued residence together under the same roof. As for Eliza, pining though she was for the sweets of independence, she had too much worldly wisdom to quit her husband without a proper settlement. Mated together thus in a humiliating bond of expediency, the two entered upon that period of their lives which was to be so decisive of their fate.

The Drapers took up their residence at Belvedere House, Mazagon. You will look in vain for any vestige of this residence in the Bombay of to-day. Some half-century ago vandalistic hands levelled the place with the ground. Time and commerce have done the rest to obliterate traces of this home of perhaps the most striking romance that Anglo-India holds. A pilgrimage to the spot will take the visitor through noisome crowded streets abutting upon a dock area abounding, as such regions do the wide world over, with squalor and dust. On the solitary hill which exists in the locality he will possibly take his stand on the exact spot where the drama of Eliza's life reached its climax, and looking around will see on one side a forest of masts, in another direction a great aggregation of chimney shafts, and elsewhere a sea of houses. No landscape scarcely could differ more than this from the one upon which Eliza's sad eyes gazed in those melancholy days of hers prior to the final separation from her husband.

Then Mazagon offered prospects which were of real beauty. Landwards there was a pleasant stretch of palm groves, whose vivid green was agreeably broken here and there by the white walls and red-tiled houses of some native grandee or perchance the spire of some Portuguese church. On the harbour side the windows of the bungalow commanded a superb view of one of the most beautiful inlets in the world. Across the turquoise-hued waters, dancing and sparkling in the tropical sunlight, the eye wandered from island to island, and island to headland, finally resting on the glorious background of the tumbled Ghaut Range, whose curious-shaped peaks suffused in a violet-tinted haze have an atmosphere of romance not belied by their history. If anywhere in India Eliza should have been happy, it was here, but she was out of tune with the music of the tropics, and, more important still, she was losing faith in herself.

There are three letters in existence relating to the early period of the life at Belvedere, and three others which have reference to the critical later days there. For the present we may confine attention to the first series, which comprises (1) a letter (No. 13 of Lord Basing's collection) dated February 6, 1772, addressed to Eliza's aunt, Mrs. Richard Sclater, now a widow residing at "the Tythings," near Worcester, with her daughter Penelope Lutley (1752–1843) and son Bartholomew (1753–1804), at this period at Worcester College, Oxford; (2) a letter to Thomas Limbrey Sclater, under date March 4, 1772; and (3) a very long communication addressed to Mrs. James (B.M. Addt. MSS. 34537), dated April 15, 1772. The first letter of the three is almost exclusively of domestic interest, but it is of value as a guide to the drift of the writer's thoughts:

DEAR Madame,—I had the pleasure of receiving your Favour by Capt. Allen and am almost ashamed to reflect that this is the first time, I have paid my Respects to you since I revisited India; Pray excuse the Omission, and be assured, I will endeavour to avoid anything like the appearance of it in future, as you have had the Goodness to assure me that an account of our Situation &

Prospects, will be pleasing to you.—I cannot say that We have any Immediate Hopes of returning to England as Independent People—

India is not what it was, my dear Madam, nor is even a very Moderate Fortune to be acquired here, without more assiduity and time, than the generality of English Persons can be induced to believe or think of as absolutely necessary. —But this Idea, painful as it is to many Adventurers who've any Notion of the difficulties they are to encounter in the road to Wealth, would not affect me considerably, if I had not some very Material reasons for wishing to leave the Climate Expeditiously. My Health is much prejudiced by a Residence in it, and my affection, for an Only Child, strongly induces me to bid farewell to it, before it's too late to receive benefit by a change of scene. Mr. Draper will, in all probability, be obliged to continue here some years longer, but as to myself, I hope to be permitted to call myself an Inhabitant of your Country, before I am two years Older, in which case, I shall have much pleasure in renewing a friendly Intercourse with a relation who has treated me with so much kindness as you formerly did My dear Madam, and in making myself beloved by my Young Cousins, whom I am told, are not only admired, for their external Merit, but exceedingly liked for the Amiableness of their Dispositions —Penelope always promised to be a charming Girl, and Report confirms the pleasing Conjectures her Youthful Appearance excited.—I request being Remember'd to her in the kindest Terms, and to My Oxonian Cousin too, May he proove as agreable a Man as his Father—and be the Pride & chief Blessing of his Mother ! then he must be as good, as He was formerly Handsome—for my dear Aunt bestows not her whole affections, but on the amiable & respectable.—

I have lately made an Acquaintance here with a very Intimate Friend of yours—a Mrs. Beet—she arrived in India about a Year ago, and has I fear been disappointed in those Golden Expectations which strangers to our Climate, generally adopt before Experience teaches them a different knowledge.—She is happy in the Circumstances of good health and cheerful Spirits—and such, I fear, are the only

Riches she ever can possess in Bombay—fortunate she will be if ever these do not desert her in a Climate so trying to European Constitutions, as that of India.—This Lady writes you herself, and therefore I shall say no more of her than that she has encreased her family lately, & seems worthy of much better fortune, than what is connected with her Situation at present.—I request my Respectful Compliments & best Wishes to Miss Lutley—Mr. Draper joins me in the same, and to yourself too, my dear Madame to whom I am with gratitude and Esteem an Obliged and most

affectionate humble servant

ELIZA DRAPER.

BOMBAY *6th Febry.* 1772.

The next letter—that to the cousin—though expressing the writer's increasing loathing for her Indian life, offers no hint of the impending disaster :

WHAT a Dear Careless Ingenuous Mortal is my beloved Cousin! you wound my Vanity but you flatter my Pride Sclater, by your forgetfulness, and honest Declarations—the former is an affront to my sex, but the latter is a Compliment to my reason, and I love you well enough to be pleased with anything which exalts your Character in my Estimation, tho' it may depreciate the Idea of my own Consequence with you at the same time.—I received your letter by, I dont know what Ship, nor does it matter much, but this I know, that I'm always pleased to hear from you, and more and more rejoiced in proportion to the length & frequency of your Epistles—if this Communication will not induce you to oblige me annually, I'm truly sorry for it, as it must give me to know, that my Consequence with you, is indeed diminish'd, if not quite lost, and that would grieve me more than I will tell you of, as without a Compliment, there is but one Person in England, whom I should more rejoice to see & be associated with than my dear Sclater.—

I am sorry that you felt inclined to like Capt. Hamilton from the circumstance of his praising me, because I think rather contemptibly of Him for the same reason too, I'm sorry, that I was in any respect the subject of his Panegyric, for I who count the Censure of Fools, Praise, am always mortified when distinguished by their approbation.—You were not Misinformed as to Drapers lucrative Post—but he has been removed from it, by the ill offices of a numerous Body, who have formed themselves into a Powerful Faction—and now, We are Adventurers again, and as much to seek for Wealth as We were the first Day of our landing Here. Our Cause must be decided at Home, and if the Directors vote against us, We have a Chance of seeing England shortly, but not in the Style of Nabobs, for Drapers Fortune will hardly admit of his ranking with a private Country Gentleman, according to the present system of Precedence.—I know not whether to Wish for Partizans, or Enemies, at the India House, for in the one Case, I have a prospect of residing many years in this Country, and in the Other, I leave it without those advantages, which alone Induces sensible People to visit it. The Conveniences of Life in Abundance, together with Indolence and the habit of being careless as to Money Matters have spoiled me for an Economical English Manager—a ruined Constitution, and *grand Despise* for the Manners & Conversation of Indians, renders me equally unfit for all the Engagements of an Eastern Society.

My inclination strongly Impels me to a Residence in your Country, and that Immediately, but when I think of the mortifying Difficulties arising from a Narrow Fortune in such a Climate as England, I own, my Resolution Staggers. Not that I think I should have any aversion to the Idea of being secluded from the World, if my Husband had those Companionable Virtues which are requisite, to banish the Dull severe, in a very retired Situation ; but He has not—this, My dear friend, your own knowledge of him, must have convinced you of,—by Nature cool, Phlegmatic, and not adorned by Education with any of those pleasing Acquirements which help to fill up the Vacuums of time agreably, if not usefully—added to which, Methodically formed, in the Extreme, by long Habit, and not easily roused into Active measures by any Motive Unconnected with his sense of Duty. Such a man, is of all Others, the least calculated to live in Retirement, when the Soul at least, ought to be awake to all the Charms of Nature, and the finer Impressions of Humanity, with a view to his making such Comparisons, as would enable him from rational Motives, to hail the rural scene, in preference to the Busy Haunts [of] Worldly Minded Men—

I love the Country, and should fix my Residence in it through Choice, if I only consulted the bent of my own Mind, but I have that in my Nature, which would render me extremely wretched in it, if my Companion had not a taste for the same Pleasures, which compose my system of Happiness.—'tis certainly the scene of all others best calculated for Wedded Lovers, of any Refinement, Understanding, or good Taste! but I much question whether it could be supportable on the present plan of Wedlocke without as great a Share of Philosophy as sensibility in the generality of Womankind, and that the prevailing mode of Education by no means Encourages.—

You talk of Moralizing, & Philosophical Disquisitions, with as much reluctance, as if they were studies beneath the Dignity of Masculine Attention—do not think so, my dear Coz,—for they mend the heart and improve the Temper, and what superior Wisdom can all the learned, all the Scientific teach? I swear to you, my Sclater, that gay, frivolous, and formed for Society as you may think me, I willingly, to be mistress of it, would live a recluse the next seven years of my life, to be enabled to pass the remainder more profitably. I love the Sages Maxims, when they are not tinctured with superstition, or those gross Enthusiasms, which dishonour the Human Character—and to be conscious of deserving the praise of Excellent Principles, with actions Morally just, and sweetly feminine (for the latter as a Woman, I could not dispense with). I, even I! with all my Volatility, would engage to serve three weird sisters, in the Persons of Maiden Aunts, with the most submissive menial attentions, tho' they were Ugly & Mischievous, as the Witches in Macbeth, provided that could Insure me such Praise, and so blend the Doctrines of Morality in my very Nature, as to make them ever the genuine Emotions of my heart in every circumstance of Active Goodness. Do you believe this ? perhaps not—but it is nevertheless true.—

and so you are Lord of Tangier & its Demesnes ! I felicitate you my Coz—and you think of taking a Wife too—I wish you a Prize, and am told, tho' not by yourself, which I take very ill, that you are likely to obtain one, in the Person of the Duke of Bolton's Daughter—is this true ? remember my dear Sclater, that I can forgive your neglecting me as a pretty Cousin, but I cannot forget your not treating me with the distinction due to a sincere Friend—How came I to hear of this Matter, if it is so, before I heard of it from yourself ? indeed I take not this kindly ! for tho' I form no Pretension to your Consideration as a Woman, I esteem myself entitled to a very material share of it as a Reasonable Creature affectionately attached to your best Interests.

As a proof that I like you much, I will ask a favor of you and confer one on you at the same time, by desiring you to get Acquainted with a Mr. George Horsley, if Chance or Design ever brings Him in your way. He now visits England, on the score of ill health—is a very intimate Friend of Ours, and very much approved by your favourite Cousin—You are not to suppose from this, that He is either Handsome, genteel, or remarkably well bred, so far from it, that He more resembles my Idea of the Knight of La Mancha than that of an Adonis or Man of fashion ;—and yet, take him, for all in all, I shall not see his like again ! therefore my dear Coz if you can be Obliging to him without Inconvenience to yourself, you will very much oblige me, and yourself too, I'll answer for it ; for you'll find Him sensible, Conversible and truly worthy—recognize your kindred kind, and he will be dear to you, as I wish an amiable friend to be, to my Dearest Relation.—

My love to your sister, she must accept it, in lieu of a letter, for as she has dropt the correspondence, I never shall revive it—I say not this in pique my Coz, but if People's Minds are so very different to each other as to be Incapable of Uttering a few reciprocal Civilities once a year without doing a violence to their Inclinations they had much better give up the farce of sympathizing at once. I wish betsey Sclater well established in Life, and such a portion of Happiness, as is most consistent with her own notions of Good.—

I am once more settled in Bombay, where I fret, pine and Languish for Ease, Health, and rational Society—the time of my Continuance in it is Uncertain, but I think I shall most assuredly leave it, by this time twelvemonth, if I am not most egregiously deceived as to my own Inclinations and Address. Draper will most probably stay Here, as long as he is permitted to do so by the Directors ; I have no ambition of the same kind. He always promised to let me return to England by the time my Girl was twelve years of age, whether he did or not, she was ten in October last, and I shall not release him from such a Promise without more altercation, than I have ever yet made use of on the same subject for I detest India, my dear Sclater, and all the Indian Tribes, and I most fervently wish, to have, the superintending my dear Child's Education before she is spoil'd as a frivolous little flirt—which is all, I think, that a Boarding school teaches grown Misses to be.—Health, Affluence, Love, Chearfulness the praises of Honor & Wisdom, be to thee, ever, my dear Cousin, I shall joy in the hearing—for most sincerely do I consider your beloved Interests, as connected with those of your Affectionate

E. DRAPER.

BOMBAY *4th March* 1772.

I never make Cop es—you must make out my Characters as well as you can. Adio !

Clearly from this letter the decisive battle had not been joined between the pair. Eliza was reckoning on a change which would allow of the realization of her almost passionate longing to be quit of India and all its "tribes." If it did not come through her husband's retirement she fully intended that it should be brought about in some fashion. Draper had always promised that she should go to England when her daughter was twelve. That pledge, she intimated to her cousin, she would not release him from without "more altercation" than she had ever made use of on the subject. Here we have a suggestion of a spirit rising in Eliza's breast which would not be quelled until its aspirations were realized. In point of fact she was rapidly reaching that stage of desperation which takes no count of the cost of a premeditated action.

The communication to Mrs. James is in some respects the most remarkable—though far from being the most attractive—of all Eliza's letters. Of prodigious length, and interspersed with anecdotes, reflections, and criticisms which are almost essays, it gives the distinct impression that the writer was not so much addressing her friend as the world at large. There are several autobiographical touches in it, personal allusions of high interest; but in the main the letter is a detached view of a world in which there are many interesting problems to be solved, mostly associated with the position of women and the upbringing of girls. It is fairly obvious that the production was an instrument Eliza employed to make the long, weary days more tolerable to her. Writing was an anodyne to an uneasy mind, distracted on the one hand by apprehension on account of Mrs. Sterne's possible action, and torn with anger on the other at the stolid opposition offered to the execution of her plans by her husband. The signs of weariness to be looked for in such a composition are not wanting. Eliza rambles on from topic to topic with little or no reference to the ordering of her matter. She wrote not a letter but a pamphlet, but it is a pamphlet which has no consistency or logical force. You read and wonder what the writer is driving at, and you end as you began in a state of perplexity as to the writer's real intention in occupying so much paper.

Still, it is a human document to be taken into serious account in the record of Eliza's life. It gives flashes of that literary genius which undoubtedly was hers, accompanied by thoughts which show her to have been an acute student of human nature, more especially that part of it which is illustrated by her own sex.

In the letter we are brought back to the dark backwater in Eliza's London career in which her communications to Sterne are floating ominously about, threatening every moment to gain publicity. Eliza's thoughts and actions from the time she heard of the novelist's decease are generally outlined. We see her at the earliest moment writing off to Becket, Sterne's publisher, offering fully to indemnify him if he will withhold from publication her letters, which she understands have been, or are to be, placed in his hands; we see her writing a letter of condolence to the daughter, offering to provide her with a home in India—we note that that offer is scornfully rejected; and we are shown Eliza raising amongst her friends subscriptions for Mrs. Sterne and Lydia, which, though disguised as compassionate aid, are plainly the price that is paid for their withholding the letters.

Throughout a greater part of the letter Eliza is occupied in justifying her action to her friend, who apparently has criticized it in several particulars, and more especially on the ground of the lack of confidence it showed in Mrs. James's devotion to her interests. Answering a reproach on this score, Eliza wrote:

YOU wonder my dear at my writing to Becket—I'll tell you why I did so—I had heard some Anecdotes extremely disadvantageous to the Characters of the Widow & Daughter, and that from Persons who said they had been personally acquainted with them, both in France and England—I had no reason to doubt the veracity of these Gentlemen Informants, they could have no view in deceiving me, or Motive of putting me on my Guard, but what arose from A Benevolence which I hope is common to the greatest part of Mankind—some part of their Intelligence corroborated, what I had a thousand times heard from the Lips of Yorick, almost invariably repeated—the Widow, I was assured, was occasionally a Drinker, a Swearer . . . & Unchaste—tho' in point of Understanding, and finished Address supposed to be inferior to no Woman in Europe—the Secret of My letters being in her hands, has somehow become extremely Public it was noticed to me by almost every Acquaintance I had in the Com(pany's) Ships, or at the Settlement—this alarmed me—for at that time I had never communicated the Circumstance, and could not suspect you of acting by me in any Manner, which I would not have acted in by myself—One Gentleman in particular told me, that both you and I should be deceived if we had the least reliance on the Honor or Principles of Mrs. Sterne, for that, when she had secured as much as she could, for suppressing the Correspondence, she was capable of selling it to a Bookseller afterwards—by either refusing to restore it to you—or taking Copies of it, without our knowledge—and therefore He advised me, if I was averse to its Publication to take every Means in my Power of Suppressing it—this influenced me to write to Becket, and promise him a reward, equal to his Expectations, if he would deliver the letters to you. I think I proposed no other Method to him except this, but I'm not sure . . . in case they were offered him for sale. . . .

She added that she was not so "fiendlike" as to desire that any woman should be proved vicious rather than virtuous, but, she went on, "it is true, my friend, I love not these ladies, and what is more I think, excuse me, my dear, that while I preserve my rectitude and sensibility I never shall." Answering a charge that she had shown a certain stiffness in her letter to her friend, more especially in addressing her formally as Mrs.

James, Eliza said that that characteristic in her communication was due to depression of spirits. Why she was depressed she related in some interesting sentences:

> You had told me that Sterne was no more—I had heard it before but this confirmation afflicted me; for I was almost an idolater of his worth, while I fancied him the mild, generous good Yorick we had so often thought him to be. To add to my regret for his loss his widow had my letters in her power (I had never entertained a good opinion of her) and meant to subject me to disgrace and inconvenience by the publication of them. You knew not the contents of these letters, and it was natural for you to form the worst judgment of them, when those who had seen 'em reported them unfavourably and were disposed to dislike me on that account.

Eliza was at special pains to disavow any ill-feeling towards Lydia or her mother. As a proof she cited the terms of a letter she had written to Colonel Campbell, in Bengal, "a great favourite of mine," who had recently raised amongst his friends six hundred rupees for the ladies' benefit, and who wished to make their acquaintance on his approaching visit to England. In her communication Eliza stated that she had heard Mrs. Sterne described as "one of the most sensible women in Europe," while Miss Sterne was supposed to have "a portion of each parent's best qualities—the sensibility and frolic vivacity of Yorick—most happily blended in her composition. Lively by nature, youth, and education, she cannot fail to please every spectator of capricious mind." But Eliza feared that "the Shandy race" would be extinct with "this accomplished young woman, for she's of the Muses train, and too much attached to them and filial duties to think of a change of name with much complacency." The clever baiting of the hook for this highly eligible bachelor, the gallant Campbell of Barbeck, Eliza took pardonable pride in.

> He has [she said] been very assiduous in collecting above one half of the money I have sent home for their use. In his profession he is supposed to have extraordinary merit, and in his principles and manners he is, I think, one of ten thousand—sensible, sweet tempered and amiable to a very great degree—added to which, lively, comical and accomplished. Young, handsome, rich and a soldier!

"What fine girl could wish more?" wrote Eliza, with a heavy note of interrogation. Then followed some remarkable words. Campbell, she said, could not be hurt by thinking favourably of the Sternes, and they might be much injured by his forming a different opinion, for the real dislike of a man of sense and honour, if formed on principle, was the severest disgrace that could happen to a woman of sentiment or reputation. "May it never be the fate of me or mine, Good Heaven, for if anything in heaven could prompt me to be guilty of suicide," concluded the writer, "it would be an affliction of this sort."

Led into an introspective vein, Eliza follows with a picture of herself as she then was. It is perhaps the most important passage in her letter:

> I am a good deal altered in my Appearance, James, since you used to view me with the Eyes of kindness, due only, to a second self—but my Head, and Heart, if self Love does not mislead me are both, much improved, and the Qualities of Reflexion and tenderness, are no bad Substitutes for that clearness of Complexion, and Je—ne—scai—quoi—dir which my flatterers used to say entitled me to the Apellation of Belle Indian. I read a great deal, I scribble much—I daily ride on Horseback bathe in the sea—and live most abstemiously—but I cannot manage to acquire confirmed Health, in this detested Country! and what is far worse, I cannot

induce Mr. Draper to let me return to England; tho he must be sensible, that both my Constitution and Mind, are suffering by the effects of a Warm Climate—I do, and must wonder, that he will not, for what good Purpose My Residence here can promote, I am quite at a loss to imagine, as I am disposed to think favourably of Mr. D's generosity and Principles My dear James, it is Evident to the whole of our Acquaintance, that our Minds are not pair'd—and therefore I will not scruple informing you—that I neither do, or will any more, if I can help it, live with him as a Wife—My reasons for this are cogent; be assured they are or I would not have formed the Resolution—I explain them not to the World—tho' I could do it, and with credit to myself; but for that very cause, I will persevere in my Silence, as I love not selfish Panegyricks—

How wretched must that Woman's Fate be, my dear James, who loving Home and having a taste for the Acquirements both Useful and Agreable can find nothing congenial in her Partners sentiments—Nothing Companionable nothing engagingly domestic, in his manner, to endear his Presence—nor anything of that Great or respectful sort which creates Public Praise, and by such means often lays the Foundation of esteem and Complacency at home—Sad! sad state! my James and Wo! to the feeling Heart so circumstanced!—a Woman who might have been a valuable Member of Society, is by such *disunion* either a mere blank—or liable to every disgrace resulting from Infamy—if finely organized—Grief and Disappointment, may render useless all her Mental Faculties—if chearful by nature and calculated to struggle with trying difficulties, in Hopes of surmounting them, these very excellences are so many snares to her as they excite to Envy, Malice & Detraction—for who is just enough to acknowledge, that an amiable sensible Woman, has fund sufficient in her own mind, to be a perpetual Resource to her in all Calamities and Exigencies—on the Contrary, who does not Insinuate, that when such a Character is unhappily pair'd, & maintains her cheerfulness, secret pleasures make her Amends, for public Penances? a thousand Causes, will rather be assigned, than the real One;

as few people are good enough themselves, for Goodness's sake, to imagine that, that Principle should regulate the Conduct of a Woman unhappily married—but surely! surely! they are mistaken—for if that same laudable affection, will not engage to the Pursuit of everything praise worthy—No other I fear, will ever bear us out—as Virtue in its comprehensive sense, to those who understand it well must have an effect in the Mind very superior to what is Excited by Inferior Principles, and yet even these, such as pride, the love of Fame, Wealth Greatness, a Honour or a Name; will sometimes enable us to forego Ease & Health —and to risque Life and Honour—and can it be so divine a Thing, to practise Worth for Glory's Sake—and equally so, at least, to practise it for its Own—when in fact this same Glory is nothing better than one of its Under Ministers?

After many divagations Eliza recurs to the subject of her hoped-for visit to England:

I shall strenuously urge Mr. Draper to let me return to England next year—that is about January next at furthest—As He always promised—that I should be with my Girl, by the time she was twelve years old, Whether He was desirous, or ready to quit India, by that time, or not—in October next, she will be eleven & I hope—I hope! Mr. Draper will not forfeit his Word to me—his Prospects, as to the Broach Affair will be then settled—and his fortune is so easy, that He may without prejudice to it, allow me four or five hundred a year, I desire no more—My Residence of Choice, would be in some one of the Villages near Town, as I mean to have Eliza intirely with me—& must be near the Metropolis—on account of the necessary Masters for her Instruction—otherwise I should have chose, to fix at some distance from London—as I know, the self Denial requisite to avoid Participation in Gay Scenes, is by no means a pleasing sensation, tho' a very necessary one, to Persons of greater taste than Affluence.—And I would at any time rather avoid Temptation, than be obliged to resist it (which I must do—if seated in the midst of it) as I have no Idea that my Philosophy is of that Invulnerable sort, which may safely defye all outward Attacks, without the least risk of endangering it—The Parthian Discipline,—to fight Flying—is the properest Method of Defence a Woman can make when Danger or Temptations assail her Courage—but to guard against their Approaches is still better Policy, as well as more Amiable—because it evinces Wisdom & Modesty too—both highly praiseworthy in the female character—and reflective of light upon each other when gracefully exerted.

The question of her daughter's education is discussed with a strong bias against boarding-schools. If she should return to England, Eliza says, she and Betsy will be as inseparable "as my right hand is from my left." She was astonished at the reasoning of those parents who imagined that a venal person would do justice to their children for the sake of a pecuniary reward:

A Boarding School may be a very proper seminary for an actress—as there she may learn to lisp before a numerous audience and to lose that Bashfulness so prejudicial to the Cause of Fame, in the way of Public Excellence—but for a Child, who is to aspire no higher, than to the Character of a private Gentle Woman, it is I think, the very worst Nursery she can possibly be fixed in—So thinking, do you not pity me James, when you connect the Idea of Betseys situation, with this plain Assurance? take into the Account too, my Dear—that all my Prospects of Worldly Happiness are dependant on the Rectitude, Manners—& Establishment of this beloved Child—Think of my being obliged to submit all these Important Concerns to Chance, and that for no better a Reason, than to remain an useless Spectator in a detestable Country, where my Health is declining, my mind tortured by the Sacrifice of my own just wishes—to a most illiberal Species of Reasoning, founded on Caprice—And then my Dear Woman, you will but do justice to my sorrow—if you think, and pronounce—that of all Beings—the most worthy your Compassion at present is your unfortunate Friend—Your almost broken hearted Eliza.—I am indeed—Unhappy!—I think,—Superlatively so!—but I will try to divest myself of this Notion,—as, with Nerves like Mine, it might accelerate a Fate, I wish to avoid, for the sake of my Dearer Self—for Betsey, would never get such another Monitress as I am Qualified to be to her—My Disappointments—real Afflictions, & natural turn of mind—all have, added to a tenderness for her, which ever, I think, was fondly Maternal—And encouraged me, to stake my last Chance for Happiness on her Head—may Heaven crown my pleased Hopes with success, and I think I shall not repine at whatever else, it's Providence imposes—

I am going to some Warm Springs of the same quality nearly, as the Bath Waters—a Bilious Complaint, obliges me to this Expedition—I wish it did not—for a change of Scene here, is attended with great Fatigue, as well as an immoderate Expence—owing to the Necessity of our carrying, Tents, Equipage, and every household Convenience along with us—I shall be absent only a Month—and yet my Expences in that time, in spite of Economy, will amount to as great a Sum, as would defray the Charges of a Voyage to England—Would to God! the Money was to be so appropriated, in preference to my Saving, and commencing "Phthisical Nymph of the Fountain."—but it will not be—and I will endeavour to rest satisfied, till, next year—

I sometimes think, my dear James—that our present Differences Here, may induce the Directors to send us a Governor from England, in preference to Appointing any of the Gentlemen Here to Succeed—in which Case, Your Commodore I suppose has a Chance of Succeeding to the Chair, if He Chooses to exert his Interest, to Obtain it—I own to you in that Case my dear, that my Wishes for seeing you accompany Him are not very Sanguine—the Climate—the Society—are dreadful Taxations, on the Mind as well as Body's Health—and I wish you to preserve Yours, Serene, and Chearful, as long as you live, and to a good old Age, without any of those Rubs & Disturbances—ill Health, & worse Spirits, usually Creates.—Your little

Maiden too—how would you dispose of her & I like not your bringing her with you, nor yet the Idea of your seperating from her, for years together—James, I think, is rather attached to this Country, See—an Instance, of the force of Habit, in this :—for absolutely, it is not otherwise to be justified on any one Principle of sound Reasoning—or Agreable Caprice—for there never was a greater Dearth, of everything which could Charm the Heart—please the Fancy, or speak to the Judgment, than what Reignes in Bombay. No Wit, Beauty, Sense, Merit, have We—nor yet Taste, Humour, Amusements—or Social Converse—And as to Worth in it's different Species, of Honor, Character—benevolence, Industry—and what is emphatically meant, by superior Abilities—We either, are too ignorant to know the real Estimation of Them—or so far degenerate, as to laugh at their ascribed Powers, when any selfish Purpose can be gratified, by the Derision of Them—Such are the People I associate with, & such must be your Fate, my dear Woman, if you Visit this Country—Happy for you—that your Mind is formed, & has that natural Biass to Goodness, which cannot now be perverted, by the Maxims, & Examples of a wretched Community—I wish you my dear Friend, all the Happiness, you can possibly wish yourself—and therefore I never wish to see you in India.—Indeed you do me but Justice in thinking that my Regard for your little Treasure, must equal the tenderness you shew towards Mine ; for 'tis certain, that I am just as sincere in wishing her Welfare, as I am in wishing that of Betseys—and I flatter myself, dear James, that these Young Plants of Ours, will not Emulate us more in any thing else, than they will in the Affection they bear to each other—for it would be a source of joy (to) me, to see them Capable of a lively friendship, and each considering the other as a second self—for which purpose, I would endeavor to instill into the mind of Eliza, how very superior the pleasure of obliging is, to that of gratifying any Inclination which has self, only, or even principally, for it's Object.—as I'm confident such a mode of thinking, must lead to the attainment of every Social Virtue, and diffuse a Complacency throughout the whole manner which would please every sensible Observer, and insure heart felt Peace, to the Possessor, of it, if any Acquisition in Nature, cou'd effect so desirable a Purpose.

There is a great deal more in the letter, but actually these passages last quoted place the whole position before us as it existed at the beginning of March 1772. The estrangement between Draper and his wife was then complete. They no longer lived together as man and wife, and they never would again if Eliza could help it. Why she took up this emphatic position she does not reveal, but it is more than to be suspected from her language that the husband had outraged her dignity by some glaring act of unfaithfulness. Later facts go to confirm this theory. It was at all events a household hopelessly divided upon the most vital principles upon which a married couple can disagree. There is a pathetic note in Eliza's sentences. She is Mrs. James's " almost broken-hearted Eliza " : she is unhappy—" superlatively so," she adds, with significant emphasis. And yet she must divest herself of her troubles lest, with nerves like hers, she might accelerate a fate she wished to avoid. What was the fate she wished to avoid ? It may have been suicide, or it may have been flight from her husband's protection. In either case it was death—physical in one, moral in the other. Poor Eliza ! Her case indeed was a pitiable one.

Chapter XI

At BOMBAY—*the* ELOPEMENT

We are now approaching the period of that momentous day in Eliza's life when she left her husband's house never to return to him. Even in the last chapter we have seen the stage almost set for that final scene in their marital tragedy. On the one side Draper, morose, obdurate, and utterly indifferent to his wife's feelings; on the other Eliza, "almost broken-hearted," "superlatively" unhappy, and sick nearly to the last stage of the life she was leading. A crisis appeared inevitable. It was probably only averted by Eliza's temporary absence from her husband on a mission of health. In her letter to Mrs. James Eliza spoke of taking the waters as at Bath, and we may assume that her destination was Dasgaon, a village in the Konkan—the low-lying strip of country below the Western Ghauts, near Fort Victoria, about sixty miles from Bombay.

Though the Dasgaon Spa no longer exists and even its memory has faded into oblivion, it was quite a popular resort with exiled Britons on the Bombay side in the last two quarters of the eighteenth century.[1] The waters there, as well as at a smaller place named Visrabhoy in another part of the Konkan, nearer to Bombay, were well adapted to the maladies of a tropical climate, and more especially to that form of *malaise* from which Eliza was obviously suffering.

[1] The invaluable Forbes gives a long description of the wells in his *Oriental Memoirs* (vol. i, p. 104).

The " cure " would have been protracted over a good many weeks, and probably the year was well advanced before the Drapers were again brought together at Mazagon.

Eliza's life at this period is for us a blank. How she occupied herself we can only conjecture. We do know, however, from her earlier letters that Bombay was a lively place in the Christmas and New Year period. Balls and receptions brought the entire European community of the higher social grade together in a pleasing intimacy. The only difference between the assemblages of that day and those of the year 1772–3 was that the latter were far larger and more pretentious. In the interval, as we have already shown, Bombay had grown enormously. Bigger in every way, the city had become of much greater importance by the additions made to the Indian Marine forces and by the increasing use made of the harbour by the ships of the Royal Navy. You have only to study the annual official lists of inhabitants prepared for the information of the directors at home to realize how substantial these accretions were. For example, in the record for 1764 no fewer than 125 names are given as those of "Marine officers, free merchants, and seafaring men in private employ at Bombay and factories subordinate." A dozen years before there were not so many names in the entire list, which included officials and women and children. The Marine element, in fact, had come practically to dominate the social life of Bombay.

With her vivid and attractive personality Eliza's society was probably much sought after by the naval men who swarmed in Bombay when the East India Squadron paid its customary call at the end of the year. In the circle of *passé* women of which the local society chiefly consisted she was, by virtue of her intellectual attainments, still "Queen," though she yet was only third or fourth on the Governor's list. It is not difficult to imagine her at the stiff and formal gatherings in the old converted monastery at Parel which constituted the Governor's country residence, holding her Court in some corner of the stately saloon in the intervals of the dance, indulging in playful badinage with the tall, good-looking fellows about her, and charming by her wit and intelligence all who were brought within range of her sprightly conversation. And we can fancy as the night wore on and the earlier stiffness relaxed some favoured courtier taking her out into the wide verandah which abuts on yonder side of the ballroom and there exchanging confidences of a strictly personal kind. The element of sentiment may have entered into them or it may not. On Eliza's side they were almost certainly the outpourings of a woman tortured beyond endurance by bonds which cut deeply into her sensitive flesh. What sailor heart could fail to be moved by such a story? Who amongst that galaxy of brave men would not be prepared to do and die in such a cause? Immoral! No doubt, from the world's standpoint, but it is not in the region of the Canon Law or of the rules of the Probate Division that the mentality of the sailor man moves. A petticoat in distress is to him ever the most touching spectacle—the one which is most potent as a lure into indiscretions. But we must say a truce to speculation on the manner in which the plot developed and proceed to deal with the plot itself.

History tells us many things, but it is often most tantalizingly silent on points of real interest. This is the case with Eliza's elopement. Reams have been written about the episode at different times; there are at least two "authentic" accounts—both different—of the manner of her elopement, and yet as regards the actual occurrence there is nothing substantial to go upon.[1] All that is known is that on the night of January 14, 1773, Eliza fled from her husband's house, and that some little time afterwards she was living under the protection of Commodore Sir John Clarke, or Clerke, whose flagship, H.M.S. *Prudent*, of 64 guns, was then in harbour. Tradition asserts that she escaped through her bedroom window and descended by a rope ladder into a boat which was in waiting below. It is a picturesque item which we need not part with lightly. The waters of the harbour then practically washed the walls of the Drapers' house. What more natural than that this avenue of escape should be used? It had the great advantage of leaving no room for interference. On land the sailor's authority might have been challenged with success; on the water hardly, with the admiral on the station playing the leading part in opposition. Still, we must fain confess that we have no warrant for that, or the even more persistent story which asserts that on quitting Belvedere Eliza was rowed on board H.M.S. *Prudent*, where she remained for some time. All that we have to go on are three letters, presently to be introduced, written by Eliza, one apparently just after the elopement, and the others before it. These documents[2] must now be allowed to

[1] In Price's *Memoirs of a Field Officer* (published 1839) there, however, is this reference to the quarrel which immediately preceded the elopement: "On the evening of Monday the 11th January occurred an altercation between husband and wife in which each, it would seem, accused the other of misconduct, Draper naming Clark and Eliza retaliating with the name of Leedes, one of her women in attendance, whom she claimed had fabricated a story against her out of jealousy. Driven to desperation, Eliza fled from Marine House on the night of the following Thursday."

[2] First published in the "Times of India" 3rd March, 1894.

speak for themselves. First comes the letter to the husband :

DANIEL Draper,—If you knew, Draper, with what anguish I accosted you at present, I think, and cannot help thinking it, that the severity of justice should give place to the sentiment of confession, in a farewell letter—I will not recriminate—I would even be all in fault, if that might serve to alleviate the disgrace inflicted on my husband, by my elopement from him ; but, Draper, be candid, I beseach you, as you sometimes can be, when it makes against yourself to be so, and then think, if you have not a great deal to reproach yourself for, in this late affair—if you can say you have not I must I fear be miserable, as my sole prospect of happiness is derived from the idea that your own consciousness will befriend me in this particular instance ; and if it does, let it operate so as to prevent your pursuing me in a vindictive manner.

I speak in the singular number, because I would not wound you by the mention of a name that I know must be displeasing to you ; but, Draper, believe me for once, when I solemnly assure you, that it is you only who have driven me to serious extremities. But from the conversation on Monday last he had nothing to hope, or you to fear. Lost to reputation, and all hopes of living with my dearest girl on peaceable or creditable terms, urged by a dispair of gaining any one point with you, and resenting, strongly resenting, I own it, your avowed preference of Leeds to myself, I myself proposed the scheme of leaving you thus abruptly. Forgive me, Draper, if its accomplishment has excited anguish ; but if pride is only wounded by the measure, sacrifice that I beseach you to the sentiments of humanity, as indeed you may, and may be amply revenged in the compunction I shall feel to the hour of my Death ; for a conduct that will so utterly disgrace me with all I love, and do not let this confirm the prejudice imbibed by Leeds's tale, as I swear to you that was false, though my present mode of acting may rather seem the consequence of it than of a more recent event.

Oh ! that prejudice had not been deaf to the reasonable requests of a wounded spirit, or that you, Draper could have read my very soul, as undisguisedly, as sensibility and innocence must ever wish to be read! But this is, too, like recrimination which I wish to avoid. I can only say in my justification, Draper, that if you imagine I plume myself on the success of my scheme, you do me great wrong. My heart bleeds for what I suppose may possibly be the sufferings of yours, though too surely had you loved, all this could never have been. My head is too much disturbed to write with any degree of connection. No matter, for if your own mind does not suggest palliatives all I can say will be of little avail. I go, I know not whither, but I will never be a tax on you, Draper. Indeed, I will not, and do not suspect me of being capable of adding to my portion of infamy. I am not a hardened or depraved creature—I never will be so. The enclosed are the only bills owing that I know of, except about six rupees to Doojee, the shoe maker. I have never meant to load myself with many spoils to your prejudice, but a moderate provision of linen has obliged me to secure part of what was mine, to obviate some very mortifying difficulties. The pearls and silk cloathes are not in the least diminished. Betty's picture, of all the ornaments, is the only one I have ventured to make mine.

I presume not to recommend any of the persons to you who are immediately officiating about me; but this I conjure you to believe as strictly true, that not one of them or any living soul in the Marine House [1] or Mazagon, was at all privy to my scheme, either directly or indirectly, nor do I believe that any one of them had the smallest suspicion of the matter; unless the too evident concern occasioned by my present conflict induced them to think something extraordinary was in agitation. O! Draper! a word, a look, sympathetick of regret on Tuesday or Wednesday would have saved me the perilous adventure, and such a portion of remorse as would be sufficient to fill up the longer life. I reiterate my request that vindictive measures may not be persued. Leave me to my fate I conjure you, Draper, and in doing this you will leave me to misery inexpressible, for you are not to think that I am either satisfied with myself or my prospect, though the latter is entirely my own seeking. God

[1] The Marine House was probably Draper's residence in the Fort.

bless you, may health and prosperity be yours, and happiness too, as I doubt not but it will, if you suffer your resentments to be subdued by the aid of true and reasonable reflexions. Do not let the false idea of my triumphing induce you to acts of vengeance I implore you Draper, for indeed that can never be, nor am I capable of bearing you the least ill will, or treat your name or memory with irreverence, now that I have released myself from your dominion. Suffer me to be unmolested, and I will engage to steer through life with some degree of approbation, if not respect. Adieu! again Mr. Draper, and be assured I have told you nothing but the truth, however it may clash with yours and the general opinion.

ELIZA DRAPER.

Next we have this letter to Horsley, the companion whom Eliza so earnestly commended to Mrs. James's attention:

DEAR Horsley,—If you knew the misery and compunction with which I addressed this to you, you would, in spite of reason and justice think me entitled to some degree of pity, though I am lost, for ever lost, to every claim which could entitle me to your esteem. This hour is my own, but whether the next may produce my death or destruction, or whatever else, heaven only knows. I dedicate it as one act of just benevolence, by requesting you to pay to Betty Mihill or her order, the sum of money which may have resulted from the sale of my diamond rings, be it what it will. Adieu Horsley! God restore you to health, and the enjoyment of yourself.

ELIZA DRAPER.

GEO. HORSLEY, Esq.

January 14, 1773.

Then, lastly, we have to introduce a letter to Eliza's faithful attendant, Mrs. Eliza Mihill:

To MRS. ELIZA MIHILL.

MY dear Betty,—This may be the last hour I may have it in my power to write or do anything of use for the benefit of you my faithful servant and dear friend; for in the latter capacity, indeed, I've rather wished ever to consider you, therefore let me dedicate it as properly as the peculiarity of my situation will admit. When Mr. Horsley went to England I consigned some few jewels to him, the amount of which would be about £500 or £600, and which I ever intended for you in case I could not induce Mr. Draper to make you a present exceeding it, and more suited to my wishes. Accept it, my dear woman, as the best token in my power, expressive of my good will to you. Do not hesitate from any point of delicacy or principle to Mr. Draper :—I am as incapable of taking mean pecuniary advantages, as the most moral persons breathing can be. This little fund, by right, is my due : it is what results from the sale of my ornaments, little perquisites due to me as a woman, and which he would never have posessed, if I had not received them ; nor will they be his, if you decline to having them—that is the worth of them. Take it then, Betty, without any scruple of conscience. The enclosed is an order on Mr. Horsley for the delivery of it to you. You will perhaps see England before me. God bless you my dear woman ! Visit my child sometimes, and speak kindly to her of her mother. My heart is full. The next twenty four hours will, in all probability, either destine me to the grave or a life of reproach—shocking alternative ; but I will endeavour to bear my fate, so as to assure my own heart. I had deserved a better, if chance had not counteracted the good propensities assigned me by nature. God give you health and a peaceable establishment in England, my dear woman. Adieu.

ELIZA DRAPER.

BOMBAY, *Marine House*, *January* 14, 1773.

What is the impression produced by these three epistles written in the thick of the crisis ? Regretfully it has to be admitted that it is that Eliza had sacrificed everything in her desperation. No other interpretation is to be placed upon her language. Her letter to her husband is a cry of anguish of a woman who has lost her all. She writes of the compunction she will feel to the hour of her death " for a conduct that will so utterly disgrace me with all I love." She would never be a tax on Draper: she would not be suspected of adding to her "portion of infamy." She asks to be left to her fate, "to misery inexpressible." She was not "a hardened or depraved creature"; she never would be. If left to herself she would "steer through life with some degree of approbation, if not respect." The other letters are couched in the same strain of self-abasement. She tells Horsley, the intimate friend of her happier hours, that she "is lost, for ever lost" to every claim which could entitle her to his esteem. "This hour," she says, tragically, "is my own, but whether the next my death or destruction, or whatever else, heaven only knows." To Mrs. Mihill she writes, apparently on the eve of her elopement, that the next twenty-four hours would in all probability either destine her "to the grave or to a life of reproach."

The cumulative force of these statements is overwhelming. Eliza was "lost," not merely in the sense that by her flight she had compromised herself irretrievably, but that she had sacrificed to the fullest extent her honour. And yet there are circumstances in this strange affair which leave an opening for doubt. If her sin had been so black as to admit of no extenuation one would suppose that she would have been absolutely cut adrift by her friends and relations. This, as the sequel will reveal, did not happen. Within a twelvemonth she was living with her uncle John Whitehill, at Masulipatam, an honoured member of his household, and writing letters in the old playful vein to her cherished cousin, Thomas Limbrey Sclater. John Whitehill was not a highly moral figure—the reverse of it, in fact—a man steeped in the vices of his class and his period; but we cannot suppose that he would have burdened himself with a niece whose shamelessness had made her name a byword in India. His constitutional selfishness, for one thing, would have guarded him against such compromising action. But even more significant than his tolerance is the maintenance of the old intimate relations with the cousin. Eliza, in her letters to be given hereafter, poses as no suppliant for mercy. She is bright, almost gay, in her gossipy talk. When she refers to past events she conveys a sense of wrong felt rather than of culpability in herself. It is all very perplexing in view of the abject terms of the letters given above. Probably the explanation is to be found in the conduct of Draper, and the widespread sympathy it evoked for the unfortunate woman—his wife. If her sin was black his was the fault because he had directly brought it about by his callous indifference and flagrant immoralities.

Draper undoubtedly was a worthy son of the father whom we have seen mentioned disparagingly in a will in connection with the upbringing of an illegitimate son. Daniel Draper also had his tale of natural children : we have the convincing evidence of his own will for that. But it would be unfair, perhaps, to place too much emphasis on this circumstance, damaging as it is to his honour. In that day, as the records abundantly prove, the second establishment was a common incident in the lives of Anglo-Indians. It penetrated down to the lowest strata of society—to the soldiers of the garrison, who left wills with bequests to female slaves, obviously their mistresses. Where Daniel Draper touched a lower depth than this conventional immorality was in harbouring in his house the woman Leedes, who was notoriously intimate with him. We may gather from Eliza's pathetic letter to her husband that it was this outrage which precipitated her action in leaving his house.

The conduct of Draper after the elopement goes to prove that he was not certain of his own ground. He seems to have commenced proceedings against Sir John Clarke, by moving the Mayor's Court at Bombay, on February 23, 1773, six weeks after the elopement, to issue a precept to hold Clarke to bail for £2000 sterling for some unspecified injury. At the next sitting of the Mayor's Court it was reported that the Sheriff was unable to execute the writ, as he was resisted by Captain Benjamin Marlow with violence, and there the matter ended. The log of H.M.S. *Prudent*, at the Record Office, shows that she remained in harbour until May 8, 1773, ten weeks after the abortive attempt to serve the writ. There was, therefore, ample opportunity for pushing the legal proceedings if Draper had been disposed to further action. But he must have come to the conclusion that he had better not go into Court. He never afterwards interfered with Eliza's movements. Indeed, he was sufficiently complaisant to leave in her custody the daughter Betsy, the only surviving child of the marriage.

Chapter XII

At Masulipatam

In the mad scramble for wealth in India in the years following the victory of Plassey Indian officialdom produced some highly disagreeable and disreputable characters. Avaricious, unprincipled, lax in morals, and often orientalized in their habits, they gave the time in which they lived in India an evil distinction which it did not lose until a generation after they had quitted the scene. They were the " nabobs " who were denounced by Burke and excoriated by Macaulay. Few liked them, and none respected them.

A typical specimen of the class was John Whitehill, with whom Eliza took refuge after her elopement. Born in 1735, Whitehill, even at the time of her taking up her residence with him, had served twenty years in India and had been involved in some important transactions not always to his credit. A characteristic episode occurred quite early in his career—in the middle of 1755—when he was on a visit to Rangoon. At that time the occupant of the Burmese Throne—the well-known king Alompra—was at war with the Pegu people. Whitehill, after paying his respects to Alompra, thought he saw substantial advantages in siding with the King's enemies. He accordingly entered into relations with them, and actually assisted to bombard the capital where he had just been hospitably received. Two years later Whitehill had the effrontery again to visit Rangoon. He was promptly seized by Alompra's people and sent up to Prome, where the King then was. Notwithstanding his previous treachery his life was spared, though his vessel, together with its cargo, was forfeited.[1] A more honourable entry in John Whitehill's record relates to his association with two other officials in the administration of Pondicherry after its capture from the French in 1761. He must have grown rich in the years immediately following, for in 1769 we find him applying to the Government for land on which to erect a country house—an extravagance against which the authorities a little later inveighed with a view to deterring their servants from following the practice.

When Eliza joined her uncle he was Chief at Masulipatam, an important administrative centre in the districts to the north of Madras—known as the Northern Circars—which had come under the control of the British Government by virtue of the settlement with Hyder Ali. The post was a highly responsible one, calling for great experience and the exercise of tact and judgment in dealing with the Indian super-landlord, who stood very much in the same relation to the cultivators as the Bengal Zemindar does to the farmers in the Eastern Presidency. Eliza, in the letter which follows, gives an interesting account of the system used in these dealings between the British and the local intermediaries. Reading between the lines of her statements in reference to revenue collection it is not difficult to understand how John Whitehill amassed the great wealth he was afterwards shown to possess. Nor need we be altogether sceptical of the estimate of Burke, in his speech on the Nabob of Arcot's debts,

[1] These transactions are all to be found related in the introduction to Symes' *Mission to Ava*.

that in the twenty years from 1760 to 1780 not much less than twenty millions of money were extracted from the Carnatic—the region about Madras—by unscrupulous officials. But Eliza's letter must be allowed to speak for itself on this and other points. It was in these terms:

I HAVE not wrote you since November last my dear Sclater, for I have not yet been furnished with the Necessary Informations from Bombay—and I know not how to write on any other subject, than that of my own very peculiar Situation. Repetitions are not only impolite, but disgusting, as they weaken the force of such arguments as derive their worth from Integrity and distress—for the one loves not Parade, and the other has too much of real Dignity annexed to it, in the Person of a Sensible Sufferer, to bear the Idea of vulgar Blandishments—Of what then should I write !—but I ought to say something and strive to convince you that I am not so selfish from serious disappointments & gloomy Prospects as to be incapable of thinking & feeling for Others.—

Are you married yet my sweet Coz ? and if not, when do you think of making the important trial ? for I cannot reconcile myself to the Idea of your living and Dying a Batchelor with so many Natural & Acquired Advantages as you are Master of :—I want to have the Family improve, as well as Increase, and it seems to rest intirely with you, whether it will do so or not, for Bess is not yoked yet, and if she was, her Progeny must be very superior to my Expectations, to answer the good work of Emendation in the Sclater line. Think not, I judge too lightly of her Merit—on the contrary I do it justice, but Discernment, which ought to award the Needs of Praise impartially, must ever give a preference to that Merit which is amiable, and attractive as well as Sterling—

Bess has great goodness of Heart, and she is not defective in Understanding but she has not sacrificed to the Graces—she is not agreable and this is a Quality indispensably requisite in the composition of a Woman, because it's necessary that our Sex should be loved as well as esteemed ;—for you Males (to whom We are by the Law of Custom or Nature, in some Measure Subservient) are not always disposed to Admire ;—in fact the Sublimities of Character have less weight with you, than the Bagatelles, when happily timed by the direction of good Sense, and good Humour ;—and in this you are as much sway'd by Wisdom as in any one of your Pursuits,—nay more, for Man as an active Being, is stimulated to excellence, either by his Wants, his Ambition, or his State in society, if Nature or Education has been at all indulgent to the Improvement of his Talents ; and this Happy restlessness so useful in the Busy Scenes of Life, naturally leads to Objects that occupy His mind intirely, and exerts his Faculties to their utmost tone, if in themselves those objects are considerable enough to speak to his Pride or affections—thus engaged in his Public Walks—His Home should be a scene of calmness and repose, He cannot support constant Agitation, and what so likely to sooth and relax his mind as the Cheerful Converse of an agreable Woman, whose manners are as much soften'd by her own Ideas of propriety, as that Home Designation appropriated to her by Custom Reason and Education ?

A Montaigne, a Pompadour or a Mrs. Cauley might perhaps excite more attention from a Courtier in a Circle than an amiably reserved English Woman with the Virtues of an Octavia, but it seldom, very seldom happens, that the Sage, the Statesman, or the mere man of Business finds his Happiness in the Society of these ;—nor, independent of Local Passion, would he choose a Companion of Genius for his Domestic Partner, for he estimates felicity, as a wise man ought to estimate it, by the Sensations of the Heart rather than the refinements of the Understanding—and for this Purpose, every woman of Principle, Sense, and good Temper, is equal to the duties of a Wife, if Nature has not been very Unkind to her appearance.—

Yes, I will maintain, and ever believe it, Coz, for the Honor of your Sex, that good Temper United with Chearfulness, and a reasonable Spirit, will ever be deemed a Cestus by the Tribe worth fixing ;—and tho' a dear bought Experience, in my own case, has not confirmed so flattering an Idea, I am as much convinced of its reality as I possibly could be of any one circumstance, to which I've not borne occular Testimony—for Reason & Nature dictate that it should be so—and what they urge must be right tho' Practise and Modern Theory should for ever controvert their Decrees.—I'm a Philosopher in Speculation my Coz—and I trust that my actions have not deviated from the Tenets of the Moral Sect, in whatever Discipline, Justice, Fortitude or Patience has exacted by way of Probation to so eminent a Degree.—I am reviled and traduced, but I am improved and you would dearly love me, my Sclater, for I deserve the love of all the Good and friendly—I will let you into my present Situation—

I live intirely with my Uncle, and I shall continue to do so to the last Hour of my Life, if he continues to wish it, as much as he does at present—He's an Extraordinary Character, Unequal but there's a great Mixture of Good I might almost say of sublime in it—for He's generous, Highly so, and literally despises Money, but as it serves to promote his Happiness—which wholly centres in his Friendships—Once attached, he is steady in these as the sun is regular in it's course,—but then He's passionate and Jealous, even to Madness—if the Objects of his regard seem to give any other Individual a temporary Preference, this is the source of extreme Misery to himself, and to all who live with Him—for the Heart—the Heart, my Coz! is a free Agent, and will at times assert its liberty of Choice in spite of the Chains imposed on it, by Gratitude, Interest or the love of ease.—In short He is one of those Beings whom his Friends would sacrifice Life or Fortune to serve or Oblige, rather than devote their whole Time to Him (be secret as the Grave, as to this Communication) and Unfortunately nothing but their time would either Satisfy or even Amuse Him.—His House, his Purse, Servants, Credit are all at their Devotion; He's pleased when We make use of them as our own, for He knows, and feels their Uselessness to Himself independent of our Participation—He's capable of all the great Exertions, to purchase Affection, but alas! He can neither relinquish his foibles, or suppress them, to secure Esteem.

Unhappy Composition ! You know not how much He distresses me, for my Obligations to Him are most important, and I wish to love Him more than any other Individual, but this, depends not on me ;—for the Heart must be won, My Sclater, and it must be fixed too by such a series of actions as secures affection on the basis of Esteem.—He now holds a most important Post, and his Fortune will be immense if He's suffer'd to remain in it five Years.—I wish he may, for I love great Objects, and everything in his Station confirms my Predilection in his favor. He has nothing to do but to follow the Dictates of Benevolence and Policy, to have his Mind most delightfully occupied. Millions might reap benefit from the former and the latter opens such a Field for Power and Emulation, as you can form no Conception of in your confined Islands—the Sea your Barrier, but He's indifferent to all such matters, his Friend, and his Neice engross all his Thoughts and his Cares—Dear, Generous, imbecile Mortals ! How I wish that the Daemons of Avarice and Ambition—or the gentle Deities of Peace and Commerce had Possession of his Mind, for then he would be happy, in having food for Employment, & our Obligations to Him, would ever secure our Love and Attention, without those cruel inroads on our Peace which at times tear the heart to Pieces, and counteract in spite of Us, our best Sensations in his Favour.—

His Friend & Premier, is a Mr. Sulivan—A sweet Character, my Coz ;—I am happy in having such a Companion for my constant associate.—He's Mild, yet Manly—a respectable understanding and a fine Disposition are his acknowledged Characteristics. So much goodness, without Parade, so much sensibility without a single foible I never before saw manifested—nor do I ever expect to be an Intimate Witness of something so near Perfection again, in any human Character. My Uncle doats on him with all the Extravagances of violent Passion—He cannot live without Him, He cannot even bear Him out of his Sight. He cannot like to have him Sleep in any apartment but his own—You cannot suppose, after what I've said that there can be any Similitude in their Tempers—You cannot imagine that the Point of Interest can sway with such a mind—Yet—how cheerfully does He submit to all Capricio's—How assiduously, under terrible disadvantages of Health, does he make himself the Slave of Business to promote Whitehill's Interest and Honor!

O, my Friend there must be a something in right and Wrong, independent of Opinion, and Sulivan must feel the whole force of its Charm! for no rule of Worldly Reasoning could enable him to deduce happiness to himself from such constant sacrifices as he must make of his Inclinations were it not that He annexed a degree of Worth to the Conduct which Morality alone, and that a very refined species of it too, can recompence him for, in the Consciousness of Acting Greatly.—How I love Dignity of Soul when it is not alloy'd by any Mixture of Ostentation—and how sincerely do I admire and Esteem a young Man of four & twenty who can thus speak to the heart and Judgement, without misleading either!—His Friendliness, his attentions, and I believe I might say his affection for myself—I rank in the Number of his Virtues—at least they are derived from the same source—and that I prize them is certain, tho' I doubt not but scandal may busy itself by vilifying me, even on his account—So erroneous are common Opinions, in their translations of Superior Sentiments.—

Conscience and a sense of Honor, I trust, will enable me to act properly in future whatever may be my Difficulties, for to those I must commit the Guardianship of my Actions —Should they fail me, I have no better resource, and tho' I would compound with Censure for a few Additional successes, rather than relinquish the Pleasure I feel in giving him every testimony of Preference in my Power, Yet I would not forfeit his Esteem for ten thousand times the Satisfaction I possess in giving him assurances of it.— This I trust, may be my security for neither trespassing the bounds of Honor or Decorum.—

We are now residing in Tents at a Place called Rajahmundry about eighty Miles from Masulipatam, Whitehill's seat of Empire—Our business Here is to settle the rents of Lands, Collections on Customs et.cra. State Matters for the next three Years.—these Lands are called Circars, an eastern Name for Provinces, and were ceded by the Subah to the Company in Consideration of the Treaty made with Him, in the close of the War with Hyder Ally.—We pay him an immense Tribute annually for holding them, but the balance I imagine is very much in our Favor, as the Circars seem to be a favorite Object with the Company, and have in general been attended with very lucrative Advantages, to the Governor and Chief.—those under Whitehills Jurisdiction are five in Number & each Commanded by a petty Prince, stiled Zemindar, who in his own District reigns absolutely, and seems every way qualified to Maintain his Power, in case He's put on the Defensive;—these Zemindars are accountable to Whitehill for the Produce of the Lands, and the Duties on Merchandize.—We raise or lower them at Pleasure, and in doing this Judiciously, consists the principal Art of our Politicks, As the Company expect an increase of Revenue from this Northern Territory annually, while it remains Undisturbed by foreign Incursions, and the Staple Commodity (Rice) for want of rain, is sometimes (as at present) so very unequal to the Consumption, that the Renter, and Husbandman find it very difficult to be punctual in their Payments to the Zemindar, who in his turn, is then at a loss, to account to the Chief and the Chief feels the weight of the Misfortune heavily, if he has not friends in the Madrass Council, and a very potent Interest in Leadenhall Street.—

There are ways, and means, to accomodate these Grievances to the Advantage of the Chief, but they are not such as a Man of Principle would embrace, as He must sacrifice his Constituent's Interest to insure his own by giving in to them.—Zemindars would always come down Handsomely, to be excused discharging their obligations to the Company for a year or two ;—and it requires not the abilities of the famous Italian Politician, to frame plausible Excuses for non-Payment, when a man is secure of enriching his own coffers by the measure—but Whitehill has no Venality of Soul.—

He will act for the best, and stand or fall by the Event.—So much for Northern Politicks.—

I have wrote to Purling, and enclos'd him a letter, which I think may be of use to my Cause if Draper continues determined to go to Extremities, it came from a Mr. Shaw, who lived with us two years as a Book Keeper—One of Drapers Children is now in England, and went there in the *Cumberland*, Capt. Savage, about thirteen Months ago—One of his Cleopatra's has signified to me, that she has no objection to swearing herself the Mother of two Children by Him, whenever I choose to have her testimony given before a Magistrate.—My Uncle will apply to a Lawyer to get it taken. My Caro Spouse has taken my Unfortunate English Woman into public keeping, and do you know that I am sorry for it as I loved the Girl, tho' in fact He could not have done anything more beneficial to my Cause, as he has thought proper to behave ridiculously enough in the Business, to lose much of his own Consequence.—I will not comment on the Justice of his Meditating a Divorce at the same time that He has no regard to Decency in his Amours—Adio! my Caro Coz—I wish you every Good—and am truely your affectionate

ELIZA DRAPER.

RAJAHMUNDRY 20*th January* 1774.

In case you get my former long letter to Mr. Purling into your Possession, I request you to inform the Newnhams & Mrs. James of its particulars.

It is a curious picture that Eliza here draws of the Masulipatam household—Whitehill, generous to profusion but almost insanely jealous in regard to the manner in which those upon whom he bestowed his largesse paid him attention; Sulivan his *fidus Achates*, quiet, submissive, almost Uriah Heepish, ministering to his exacting needs; and Eliza flitting about in the background, causing, one may suspect, many flutterings of heart in the susceptible Sulivan, and exciting the frowns of the great man for daring to attract to herself any share of the devotion which by undeniable right was his. Whitehill's probably was only an extreme case of that form of aberration not infrequently met with in the ranks of the vulgar rich: that monetary payments justify the exaction of the widest measure of homage and personal sacrifice from dependents. But whether so or not he is distinctly shown as a man with whom it was difficult, if not impossible, to live.

Still, Eliza clearly was not unhappy in these Masulipatam days. If she did not tell us how much she was improved in condition we should gather it from her unrestrained flow of talk as she communes in her own peculiar fashion with her beloved "coz." A great weight appears to be off her mind. She is no longer the sinner whose sin is too grievous ever to enable her to face the world again, but a woman who may be vilified but has no sort of intention of submitting tamely to such treatment. The explanation, as we have before said, probably is that she is now sure of the sympathy of those whose opinions are most to her. She would not be writing to Thomas Limbrey Sclater if that young gentleman had not taken good care to let her know directly or indirectly that he thought her a much-wronged woman. Mrs. James's support also had evidently been obtained or there would not be the friendly reference there is to her in the postscript of the letter. Clearly Eliza had been fighting her case with considerable success with the powerful aid of her uncle. The statement sent to Purling, the Chairman of the Court of Directors, was a justification which must have carried weight if the evidence furnished of Draper's immoralities was of the damning character of that outlined in the letter. In the circumstances there was reason for Eliza's high spirits. She was a somewhat spotted innocent, perhaps, but still not the fallen creature which she had been pictured, and which she had pictured herself a twelvemonth previously.

Though Eliza, with a loyalty which we can understand and commend, would permit herself to say nothing to her uncle's disadvantage, she makes it clear that the situation is becoming an impossible one. History is silent as to when the queer combination she sketched broke up ; nor do we know in what circumstances she left her uncle. All that is certain is that at the close of 1774 she was in England again. How she must have rejoiced to be in the beloved homeland once more, in touch with those nearest and dearest to her! And yet not without satisfaction would it have been to Eliza's sentimental mind if she had known that long years after her passing from the scene the memory of her sojourn at Masulipatam would have been literally kept green by a tree under which she was in the habit of sitting, and which by that fact became known as "Eliza's tree." Concerning this tree Mr. J. J. Cotton, C.S., writes :

> While at Coonoor in the hills I met an old woman, Mrs. Marjoribanks by name, who remembers Eliza's tree and Masulipatam. It was blown down in the cyclone of 1864, in which Mrs. Marjoribanks's own mother lost her life. The tree is said to have been a cedar tree and the only tree of any dimensions in the station. It was a favourite rendezvous for people to sit under. Mrs. Marjoribanks lived at Masulipatam, or Bandar as it was always called, from 1851 to 1869 and remembers the tree perfectly.

John Whitehill fades out of Eliza's life at this stage, but we must not part with him with a simple curt word of farewell, for, taken all in all, he was the most extraordinary figure in the whole story outside the leading characters. Very soon after Eliza left him, towards the close of 1776, he proceeded to England on leave on private affairs. While he was at home an astounding *coup d'état* occurred at Madras by which the ruling Governor, Lord Pigot, was dethroned and imprisoned, and power usurped by a faction led by George Stratton, the husband of Hester Light, Eliza's cabin companion.

When the news of the occurrence reached England the directors were naturally anxious that their authority should be reasserted at the earliest possible moment. Whitehill presenting himself as a suitable envoy for this purpose, was entrusted by them with the mandatory despatch, and travelling expeditiously via Suez he reached Madras on August 31, 1777, only 79 days after leaving London. In the meantime Lord Pigot had died in imprisonment. His death was due to natural causes, but it was undoubtedly accelerated by the treatment he had received. Whitehill, finding himself the sole member of the Provisional Government on the spot, took action. Having assumed the Governorship, he addressed what was tantamount to an ultimatum to the usurpers. This brought about their submission, but though a verdict of murder was delivered by a coroner's jury in regard to Lord Pigot's decease nothing came of it.

Whitehill retained the Governorship from August 31, 1777, until February 8, 1778, when Thomas Rumbold, the senior Councillor, who had been nominated for the office, arrived and took over charge. The new reign did not last long. Rumbold soon got into trouble with Hyder Ali, the Nizam, and the Supreme Government, and on April 6, 1780, he handed over the reins to Whitehill again and sailed for England. The cause which brought Rumbold to grief led a few months later to Whitehill's downfall. Towards the end of the year Hyder Ali again erupted into the Carnatic and devastated the country almost to the walls of Madras. Whitehill, quite unprepared for the onslaught, made but a feeble defence, and sent urgent messages to Calcutta for assistance. In response to his appeal Sir Eyre Coote was despatched to Madras with a body of troops, and by the orders of Warren Hastings, who was then Governor-General, Whitehill was suspended. Subsequently, by an order of January 10, 1781, this action was confirmed, and Whitehill and his two recent associates in the Government, Sir Thomas Rumbold and Perring, were dismissed the Company's service.

The later Parliamentary proceedings are part of the political history of the time. The House of Commons appointed a Secret Committee under the chairmanship of Henry Dundas to investigate the affairs of the Carnatic, and on April 9, 1782, Dundas moved that the reports from this Committee should be considered by the whole House. A bill of pains and penalties was subsequently introduced against Rumbold, Whitehill, and Perring. It passed a second reading at the end of the Session, but owing to changes in the Government and to other matters of more immediate interest the bill was dropped during the following Session.

Even this does not end the strange eventful history of John Whitehill. According to a Calcutta paper, the *India Gazette* of July 13, 1782, he was obliged to fly to France in order to save his life, there being strong suspicion that he was part-owner of a French privateer which had captured the East Indiaman *Osterley* off Mauritius some time previously. Whitehill is said to have been accompanied in his flight by the fascinating

Mrs. Grand,[1] who afterwards, as the wife of Talleyrand, Napoleon's famous Minister, was so conspicuous a figure of the Revolutionary period. A scandalous chronicle of that eventful time,[2] written by an Englishman named Goldsmith, supplies some piquant details of this association. How far his account of Mrs. Grand and John Whitehill is true it is difficult to make certain of, but it may be noted that Mr. Busteed, in the last edition of his *Echoes of Old Calcutta*, makes Mr. Thomas Levin, a young Madras civilian and a friend and supporter of Whitehill, the hero of the episode. Mr. Busteed, however, apparently never came across Goldsmith's work. It is almost certain that the date 1786 given as that of the voyage home of Mrs. Grand is a mistake. From independent sources we know that she left India at the end of 1780, and that Whitehill sailed about the same time.

Goldsmith's story is to the effect that Whitehill, "having amassed a very considerable fortune in India," lavished it on Madame Grand. "He bought an hotel for her, furnished it in most magnificent style, purchased jewels to the amount of £20,000 sterling, and bought in the French funds a life annuity for her of 30,000 livres per annum, about £1200 sterling." Afterwards Madame Grand found other admirers and,

[1] Madame Grand was born at Tranquebar, November 21, 1762, the daughter of a Dane, M. Peter John Worlee, Captain of the Fort of Chandemagore. She married, July 10, 1777, George François Grand, of the Indian Civil Service, then Secretary to the Salt Committee and head assistant and examiner in the Secretary's Office. In February 1779 Grand brought an action against (Sir) Philip Francis for criminal conversation on December 8 with the wife of the plaintiff, and after trial before Impey, C.J., and Chambers and Hyde, J.J., obtained on March 6, 1779, a judgment in his favour and 50,000 *sicca* rupees as damages, and later a divorce from Mrs. Grand; she lived at Hughli under Francis's protection in 1779, and went to Europe in 1780–1 (*Dictionary of Indian Biography*).

[2] *Secret History of the Cabinet of Bonaparte*, 2nd edition (1810), p. 539.

Chapter XIII

In England *Again*—Last Days

Not many months after writing the letter given in the previous chapter, certainly not later than the end of 1774, Eliza was back in England—her England—the land she loved so well. She was still only a little over thirty years of age, but bitter experiences had been hers since she last set foot on English soil. She had been through the furnace and had come out of it with scorched wings. Physically she was still " La Belle Indienne "—a little delicate, perhaps, with traces of care about those full expressive eyes we have read about, but on the whole the same fascinating creature that she was of old time.

Things, however, for her could never be the same again. Sterne was a considerable literary figure, and the fame, or otherwise, of the old Gerard Street intimacy had been spread abroad through the medium of *The Sentimental Journey*, which had already by this time become a classic. Some drawing-rooms at least would have been closed to the heroine of the Belvedere episode, if not to " the Bramine " of the Bond Street idyll.

Whether Mrs. James continued her friend to the extent of receiving her we do not know. She could hardly have done so, perhaps, in the circumstances in which her husband was then placed as a leading light at India House and a rising public man. Draper had friends in the Leadenhall Street quarter, and with according to Goldsmith, abandoned him in his old age to a degrading life of poverty. The last picture we have of him is as "an old man upwards of eighty years of age without a sous," supplicating Madame Grand for relief, and ultimately obtaining from her a compassionate allowance of £60 per annum to defray his board and lodging. Such is the account of the end of Eliza's protector of Masulipatam. There is nothing intrinsically improbable in it. It at least rounds off with dramatic finish a career which presented many ignoble features.

unrestrained intercourse awkward incidents might have occurred. So we may fairly assume that Eliza lived a somewhat retired life, cultivating the quieter joys of the fireside in those first winter evenings after her return from India.

According to a veracious authority—Wilke's list of addresses—Eliza, in December 1774, was in residence at 3 Queen Anne Street, Cavendish Square. This was not only a fashionable locality; it was a famous literary centre. In 1760 Burke had removed there from Wimpole Street, "next door to Mr. Fitzherbert." A few months after Eliza went into residence she had as a neighbour Edward Malone, the Shakespearian commentator. Here also resided Richard Cumberland, the playwright, and here was probably written his best play, *The West Indian*. Memories of the famous Dr. Busby, of Westminster School fame, cling to the street, but its greatest tradition, perhaps, is associated with the ineffable and inimitable Boswell, who took a house in the thoroughfare while his *Life of Johnson* was passing through the press. The mere fact of Eliza's residing in such a street shows that she had considerable social resources.

It must have been while Eliza was living in Queen Anne Street that the arrangements were carried out for the publication of Sterne's letters to her. They were issued, doubtless with her sanction, under the following title:

> Letters from Yorick to Eliza. London: Printed for G. Kearsley at No. 45 in Fleet Street; and T. Evans, near York Buildings, Strand, 1775.

The volume is dedicated to the "Rt. Hon. Lord Apsley, Lord High Chancellor," and it contains an introduction of a general character, adducing no new fact of importance in connection with Eliza's life. The dedication, however, is of exceptional interest from several standpoints. Lord Apsley was the son of the aged Lord Bathurst, the friend of Sterne, who had enthusiastically toasted Eliza's health on the occasion referred to in an earlier chapter. The Lord Chancellor was a dour, somewhat ascetic individual, offering a striking contrast to his extremely sociable and jovial father; so much so, says Campbell,[1] "that when, after supper, the son had retired, the father would rub his hands and say to the company, 'Now that *the old gentleman* is gone to bed, let us be merry and enjoy ourselves.'" It was this Lord Apsley who, when at the Bar in 1752, prosecuted Miss Bland for the murder of her father at Oxford—a crime which was one of the great *causes célèbres* of the century. But, according to Campbell, "the most memorable act in his life was that he built Apsley House at Hyde Park Corner, the town residence of the illustrious Duke of Wellington—where stood 'The Hercules Pillars,' the inn frequented by Squire Western." There is no need to labour the point that the association of such a man with Eliza's literary venture, even though merely through the unsubstantial link of a dedication, is conclusive that her status at the time was good.

Scarcely the same odour of respectability attached to another prominent acquaintance she made at this juncture—John Wilkes. How or when the demagogue became acquainted with Eliza is not absolutely clear, but it is fairly safe to assume that the connection grew out of the publication of Sterne's letters. Sterne had been associated with Wilkes in some of the rather dubious byways of social life of an earlier period, and

[1] *Lives of the Lord Chancellors*, vol. vii, p. 120.

it was natural that he should be more than ordinarily interested in productions which gave a profound insight into the novelist's views and mode of life. It is quite possible that the tie was formed through the agency of the publisher. Wilkes at that juncture was at the summit of his extraordinary career. He had just been elected Lord Mayor amid the delirious enthusiasm of the populace, and he had taken his seat in the House of Commons after having been banned from the popular assembly for eight years. His imprimatur on a book of the character of *Yorick's Letters to Eliza* would, therefore, be of exceptional value. Whether sought or not, it seems to have been given with unusual warmth, judging from the tenour of the following undated letter from Eliza to Wilkes which has come down to us :[1]

I THANK you, for the french Volume, Mr. Wilkes, and I really feel myself obliged for the english Pages, tho' the elogium which accompanied them makes me half afraid of indulging a something, which I presume to call taste, for the pleasure of Wit, and Conversation ; as, there is nothing which I ought to be more apprehensive of than Praise, from distinguished Persons, because it ever has had too powerful an effect on my imagination to render me capable of aspiring to Merit, in capital Instances—I say not this, with a view to disqualify and extort refinements or flattery, but from such a consciousness of my own imbecility as makes me very serious, when reduced to the necessity of self examination—if therefore, you have the generosity, which I take you to have, you will rather endeavour to correct my foibles than to add to it by your encomiums—I request my compliments, if you please to Miss Wilkes, and am your much obliged, and most Obedient

ELIZA DRAPER.

Sunday Afternoon, *March* 22*nd*.

[1] *Wilkes MSS*. 30875, vol. ix, p. 112.

From this communication we can gather that the intimacy went beyond a merely formal exchange of literary compliments. Eliza had had a call from Miss Wilkes—the demagogue's beloved daughter " Polly " —a sure mark of the father's exceptional interest in the person honoured by the attention. It has been suggested that with his usual love of libertinage Wilkes sought to give the acquaintance a more ardent character, and was only restrained by Eliza's good sense. Nothing is more probable than that this was the actual state of affairs, but there appears to be no real evidence to warrant the statement. Wilkes merely drops out of the story as others have done, because his subordinate part in it has been fully played.

What seems to have happened was that Eliza moved about a good deal in the literary coteries of the day, attracting unusual attention by her striking personality and her picturesque, if compromising, antecedents. In this way a good many men of note had a more or less close acquaintance with her. By a number of these she was strongly urged to give to the world some of her own literary compositions, more particularly her letters to Sterne. Eliza, however, resolutely declined to listen to these overtures. Apart from diffidence as to her literary capacity, she probably had a strong distaste for publishing to the world the proofs of her intimacy, innocent though she knew herself to be of any worse failing than indiscretion. But what she was not prepared to do for herself others were ready to do for her. Some time afterwards there appeared in print a volume entitled *Eliza's Letters to Yorick.* It was an impudent forgery, coined, it is believed, by William Combe, a rather notorious literary character of that time, who is best remembered to-day by the authorship of that whimsical work, *Dr. Syntax*. Combe may have been snubbed by Eliza at some period or other. Anyway, it is difficult to account otherwise for a coarse slander he circulated in reference to her. The story, which is to be found in the well-known work [1] recording the table talk of Samuel Rogers, is to this effect :

> Combe assured me [i.e. Samuel Rogers] that it was with him, and not with Sterne, that Eliza was in love; that he used to meet her often inside a windmill near Brighton; and that he was once surprized in her bedchamber, and fled through the window, leaving one of his shoes behind him; that, some days after, he encountered her as she was walking with a party on what is now the Steyne [at Brighton], and that as she passed him she displayed from her muff the toe of his shoe.

It is hardly necessary to attempt to refute this precious legend. Obviously it is the product of a low mind bent on notoriety, and in addition personally biased against the unfortunate victim of its venom.

Turn we now to what, next to the Sterne friendship, is the greatest literary episode in Eliza's life—her intimacy with the Abbé Raynal. Properly to understand this association we must carry our minds back to the era in the latter portion of the eighteenth century, in which the Abbé moved as a highly popular figure. Though almost, if not quite, forgotten to-day his *Histoire Philosophique et Politique des Établissements et du Commerce des Européens dans les deux Indes* excited enormous interest in the period following its first publication in 1770. The writer, who had been brought up as a priest, and who was expelled from the Jesuit Order to which he belonged in 1748, in his work strongly eulogized British methods and enter-

[1] *Reminiscences and Table Talk of Samuel Rogers*, Powell's edition, p. 80.

prize in the East and West Indies, and sympathetically dealt with the entire British policy of colonization.

Angered at the backing given to a formidable rival of its schemes, the French Government ordered the Abbé's volumes to be publicly burnt. In England precisely the contrary reception was accorded to the work and its writer. The History was on the table of every person of distinction, and when the Abbé on one occasion visited the House of Commons the Speaker paid him the rare honour of suspending the sitting temporarily in order that he might be provided with a good place. At about the same time—in 1778—the Abbé was elected a Fellow of the Royal Society. The critical state of the times—the loss of the American Colonies was a poignant recent memory—no doubt lent fervour to these compliments. It was a salve to the sorely wounded national pride to have at hand the impartial testimony of the Abbé to the excellence of the British Colonial system.

Probably it was on the occasion of this visit to London in 1778 that the Abbé became really intimate with Eliza. He had met her previously a good many years before in Bombay, and if we are to trust his word his soul instantly took flame at contact with so ethereal a being. It was not passion ; it was not love ; it was, the Abbé said, " a sensation unknown to me." Whatever name we may apply to the Abbé's indeterminate feelings, we can have no doubt as to their potency. He wrote on Eliza a threnody which, for sustained and almost delirious sentiment, has hardly any equal, even in the French language, in which it is written. Though it more properly belongs to the latest period of the story, it may be introduced here. By way of preface, however, it should be explained that the first edition of

GUILLAUME THOMAS FRANÇOIS RAYNAL

the Abbé's History, which was anonymous, was published at Amsterdam in 1770, in 4 vols. 8vo., and contained no allusion to Eliza. Subsequent editions appeared, also without any such reference, and then came in 1780 the great edition published under Raynal's own name at Geneva, in 10 volumes, in which there is an account of the kingdom of Travancore embodying the famous rhapsody on Eliza. A translation of this appeared in the *European Magazine*,[1] and it may be given here as an admirable English interpretation of the text :

Territory of Anjengo, thou art nothing ; but thou hast given birth to Eliza. A day will come when these staples of commerce, founded by the Europeans on the coasts of Asia, will exist no more. Before a few centuries are elapsed, the grass will cover them or the Indians, avenged, will have built upon their ruins. But if my works be destined to have any duration, the name of Anjengo will not be obliterated from the memory of man. Those who shall read my works, or those whom the winds shall drive towards these shores, will say : There it is that Eliza Draper was born ; and if there be a Briton among them, he will immediately add, with the spirit of conscious pride, And there it was that she was born of English parents.

Let me be permitted to indulge my grief, and to give a free course to my tears ! Eliza was my friend. Reader, whosoe'er thou art, forgive me this involuntary emotion. Let my mind dwell upon Eliza. If I sometimes moved thee to compassionate the calamities of the human race, let me now prevail upon thee to commiserate my own misfortune. I was thy friend without knowing thee ; be for a moment mine. Thy gentle pity shall be my reward.

Eliza ended her days in the land of her forefathers, at the age of three-and-thirty. A celestial soul was separated from a heavenly body. Ye who visit the spot on which her sacred

[1] Vol. v, 1784, pp. 171–3.

ashes rest, write upon the marble that covers them : In such a year, in such a month, on such a day, at such an hour, God withdrew his spirit, and Eliza died.

And thou, original writer, her admirer and her friend, it was Eliza who inspired thy works, and dictated to thee the most affecting pages of them. Fortunate Sterne, thou art no more, and I am left behind, I wept over thee with Eliza ; thou wouldst weep over her with me ; and had it been the will of Heaven, that you had both survived me, your tears would have fallen together upon my grave.

The men were used to say, that no woman had so many graces as Eliza : the women said so too. They all praised her candour ; they all extolled her sensibility ; they were all ambitious of the honour of her acquaintance. The strings of envy were never pointed against unconscious merit.

Anjengo, it is to the influence of thy happy climate that she certainly was endebted for that almost incompatible harmony of voluptuousness and decency, which diffused itself over all her person, and accompanied all her motions. A statuary who would have wished to represent Voluptuousness, would have taken her for his model ; and she would equally have served for him who might have had a figure of Modesty to display. Even the gloomy and clouded sky of England had not been able to obscure the brightness of that aerial kind of soul, unknown in our climates. In everything that Eliza did, an irresistible charm was diffused around her. Desire, but of a timid and bashful cast, followed her steps in silence. Any man of courteousness alone must have loved her, but would not have cared to own his passion.

I search for Eliza everywhere : I discover, I discern some of her features, some of her charms, scattered among those women whose figure is most interesting. But what is become of her who united them all ? Nature, who has exhausted thy gifts ? Didst thou make her to be admired for one instant, and to be for ever regretted ?

All who have seen Eliza, regret her. As for myself, my tears will never cease to flow for her all the time I have to live. But is this sufficient? Those who have known her tenderness for me, the confidence she had bestowed upon me, will they not say to me, She is no more, and yet thou livest ?

Eliza intended to quit her country, her relations, her friends, to take up her residence along with me and spend her days in the midst of mine. What happiness had I not promised to myself ? What joy did I not expect, from seeing her sought after by men of genius ; and beloved by women of the nicest taste ? I said to myself, Eliza is young, and thou art near thy latter end. It is she who will close thine eyes. Vain hope ! Fatal reverse of all human probabilities ! My old age has been prolonged beyond the days of her youth. There is now no person in the world existing for me. Fate has condemned me to live and die alone.

Eliza's mind was cultivated, but the effects of this art were never perceived. It had done nothing more than embellish nature ; it served in her, only to make the charm more lasting. Every instant increased the delight she inspired ; every instant rendered her more interesting. Such is the impression she left in India ; such is the impression she made in Europe. Eliza then was very beautiful ? No, she was simply beautiful ! but there was no beauty she did not eclipse, because she was the only one that was like herself.

Eliza has written ; and the men of her nation, whose works have been most abounding in elegance and taste, would not have disavowed the small number of pages she has left behind her.

When I saw Eliza, I experienced a sensation unknown to me. It was too warm to be no more than friendship ; it was too pure to be love. Had it been a passion, Eliza would have pitied me ; she would have endeavoured to bring me back to my reason and I should have completely lost it. Eliza used frequently to say, that she had a greater esteem for me than for any one else. At present I may believe it.

In her last moments Eliza's thoughts were fixed upon her friend ; and I cannot write a line without having before me the monument she has left me. Oh ! that she would also have endowed my pen with her graces and her virtue !

Methinks, at least, I hear her say, " That stern muse that looks at you, is History, whose awful duty it is to determine the opinion of posterity. That fickle deity that hovers o'er the globe, is Fame, who condescended to entertain us a moment about you ; she brought me thy works, and paved the way for our connection by esteem. Behold that phœnix immortal amidst the flames ! it is the symbol of Genius, which never dies. Let these emblems perpetually incite thee to shew thyself the defender of humanity, of truth and of liberty."

Eliza, from the highest Heaven, thy first and last country, receive my oath : I swear not to write one line in which thy friend may not be recognised.

In this impassioned appreciation of Eliza's virtues and talents we have a measure of the extraordinary influence she exercised over Raynal, as over Sterne. If we are to accept in their literal sense some of the statements made by the Abbé, there existed an understanding between them that they were to enter upon a closer union than simple friendship allows, when the death of Eliza put a veto upon their plans. A letter written by Raynal, in which the writer made a definite proposal that Eliza should make a home with him in France, lends a certain colour to his assertions. But it is highly probable that no such arrangement as that indicated was ever made or even seriously contemplated by Eliza. As in the case of Sterne, Raynal allowed his imagination to run riot in a picture of his declining years solaced by the presence of one so gifted and attractive as was this companion of his hours of fame. But it remained a sheer phantasy. Eliza was of an age and experience to know the inevitable consequences of such a connection. She had paid the heavy price of one false step : she was not at all likely to incur the penalty of another and more serious departure from the moral and social code. So on the balance of probabilities we may relieve the memory of Eliza of this last stain.

A heavy veil obscures the events of the last days of Eliza's life. All that we know with certainty is contained in the bald announcement which appeared in *Felix Farley's Bristol Journal* of August 8, 1788: "The same day (i.e. August 3rd, 1778) died at Clifton Mrs. Eliza Draper." A Bristol historian asserts that she died at the residence of her kinsman, Sir William Draper, the famous general, who at the time is known to have had a house at Clifton. On what authority the statement is made, if any beyond local conjecture based on a natural inference, we do not know. The records, if such existed, have long since disappeared. The fact that Eliza was buried within the precincts of the Cathedral—in the north aisle of the choir, where a diamond-shaped stone on the floor marks her grave—lends, however, substance to the story that in her last days she was taken under the care of the old soldier. Such sepulture would not have been for the poor and friendless. Nor in such circumstances would there have been erected to her memory the elaborate monument by Bacon, a popular sculptor of the time, which is now to be seen in the cloisters, but which was originally placed on the west wall of the church, where it remained until the restoration of the church, involving the removal of the wall, necessitated the transfer of Bacon's work. This memorial bespeaks an unmistakeable dignity in the conditions in which Eliza was placed when death ended her troubled career. It consists of a plain basement supporting a pointed arch of Siena marble. Under the latter, standing on each side of a pedestal bearing an urn, are two female figures of white marble in alto-relievo, meant to personify Genius and Benevolence, and a bird in the act of feeding its young, said to be an attribute of the latter virtue. The inscription runs as follows : " Sacred to the memory of Mrs. Eliza Draper, in whom Genius and Benevolence were united. She died August 3rd, 1778, aged 35."

Who was at the expense of this costly tribute of remembrance is one of the many mysteries of Eliza's history. The most obvious inference from the facts as they are known is that the Abbé Raynal was responsible for the work being set up. The sentiment it expresses is certainly his, even though the words of the inscription but poorly represent his fervid admiration of the subject of the memorial.

Eliza's daughter Elizabeth, the Betsy of the correspondence, survived her. On October 1, 1785, she married Thomas Nevill, and by him had one son and three daughters, who are all mentioned in the will of their grandfather, Daniel Draper. Draper himself enjoyed remarkable longevity. After rising to the position of Second in Council in Bombay, he retired in 1782 with the goodwill of the Court of Directors expressed in a cordially worded minute. The possessor now of a handsome fortune, he acquired an estate at Great Stanmore, Middlesex, where he for the most part resided until his death, which occurred on March 20, 1805, at his town house in St. James's Street, London. In accordance with his wishes he was buried at Great Stanmore, where his grave, covered by a flat stone and surrounded by railings, is still to be seen. On the stone is this inscription : " This tomb is dedicated in pious regard to the memory of Daniel Draper, Esq., who departed this life March 20, 1805, in the 77th year of his age." By his will Draper left bequests amounting to nearly £100,000 to his nieces and to his grandchildren (Eliza's offspring), making Rawson Hart Boddam his executor. Rawson Hart Boddam himself was, at the time, in retirement, after a very distinguished Indian career culminating in the Governorship of Bombay, which he held from January 1, 1783–4, to January 9, 1787–8, when he quitted India. He had the distinction of being the first Governor who was paid entirely by salary, his emoluments amounting to the handsome sum of nearly £10,000 per annum. After his return home he settled at Capel House, Bull's Cross, near Enfield, Middlesex. He married for a second time, Eliza Maria Tudor, a niece of Daniel Draper, by whom he had a large family of nine children, to all of whom Draper left legacies. He died at Bath in 1812. His portrait is now in the possession of Mrs. Hungerford Meyer Boddam, of Capel House, Guildford.

In this connection there remains to be traced the history of the branch of the Boddam family which descended from Eliza's sister Mary, the unhappy girl-wife of an earlier chapter. Mary Boddam's only child, Charles Boddam, was born in 1762, and was probably sent home early in life to be educated. He returned to India in 1780, having been appointed a Writer for Bengal. He held various appointments in Behar, and was, in 1793, "senior merchant and judge of the Dewanee Adawlet, and magistrate of the Zillah of Sarum." He died in Calcutta, August 13, 1811.

Charles Boddam married, in 1796 (*Gents. Mag.*, p. 1055), Charlotte, daughter of "Col. Barrington, who fell on the Continent," by whom he had a son, George Rawson Boddam, and two daughters, mentioned in his will dated 1805.[1] Of these the son, George Boddam (1797?–1824), went out to India in 1819 as an Ensign in the 48th Madras N.I., and died in 1824 at Cuddapah. One of the daughters married a Mr. Lisle Hall, and died about 1869.

A few final sentences in this biographical survey must be devoted to the James's, with whom Eliza was so intimate. Commodore James's wealth procured for him a seat on the board of directors of the East India Company, of which at different times he was chairman and deputy chairman. He was for a period M.P. for West Looe, in Cornwall, an Elder Brother of Trinity House, and was, on July 25, 1778, created a baronet. He died suddenly of apoplexy at the festivities in connection with his daughter's wedding on December 16, 1783. His widow in 1784 erected in his honour a tower on the top of Shooter's Hill, which still stands, as a memorial of his successful career. She died August 9, 1789, and as six years later the only son of the marriage was also removed by death the title became extinct. A fine portrait of Commodore James by Sir Joshua Reynolds perpetuates the features of a remarkable man whose friendship with the Drapers had a strong influence in determining the lines of the fate of the unfortunate Eliza.

* * * * *

[1] In Charles Boddam's will are also mentioned two MS. volumes of Indian Mythology which he spent ten years in translating from Persian into English; these passed from his daughter, Mrs. Lisle Hall, to Miss E. Muriel Boddam, of Capel House, Guildford, a great grand-daughter of Rawson Hart Boddam by his second marriage. The title of the volumes is as follows:—"The Adhy Atma Ramayan of Vyasa: a history of the seventh Incarnation of Vishnu. Translated from the Sanscrit into Persian by Anand G'han, a member of the College of Brahmins at Benares. And again translated from the Persian into English. In two volumes. MDCCCIV." The introduction is dated Chuprah, December 18, 1804; the work is in two stout bound volumes and is illustrated by a number of fine coloured plates by Indian artists.

Though nearly a century and a half has passed since the grave closed over the remains of Eliza, her name still lives in English literature. Hers is no doubt a reflected glory, and a somewhat tarnished glory at that. But the interest in her life history is real, and she takes her place with others who have lived their brief day in the light of genius in circumstances which have not escaped the condemnation of the censorious. How far in her case the adverse criticism of moralists was justified is a problem upon which opinion will probably ever be divided. In recent times Thackeray's savage denunciation of Sterne in his *English Humourists* has exercised a dominating influence on men's minds greatly to Eliza's detriment. True, the great novelist's barbed shafts were directed exclusively against " the foul satyr," "the wretched, worn-out old scamp," " the coward," as he successively called Sterne. Nevertheless, he clearly involved Eliza in his censure albeit he represented her as " the poor foolish Bramine " who fell a victim to the wiles of a base deceiver.

We have already dealt with this phase of Eliza's history and need not traverse the ground anew. Suffice it on that point to reaffirm the opinion that the evidence available in Sterne's letters and Eliza's own correspondence and the probabilities are opposed to the more serious view of the intimacy.

In charity we may leave these moral questions to sleep with others of the unsolved personal riddles of literary history, and regard her simply as a woman who has left her mark on English literature. Viewed in this light we may find her more than the heroine of some dubious episodes, or even the *belle esprit* who helped to brighten some idle hours of greatness. Sterne's high opinion of her literary gifts, though coloured with the insincerity with which he invested all his relations with women, was, it would seem, genuine. When he told her how sweetly she wrote he paid no empty compliment. There is a charm in her letters which lends them undeniable distinction. She writes with a vivacity and lightness of touch which few of her time excelled. In some of her letters there is a distinct suggestion of Lady Mary Wortley Montagu—a suggestion which is probably not accidental, as the famous letters of that brilliant writer, first published in 1763, were the fashionable reading in the period covered by Eliza's married life. Where Eliza fails is in her more ambitious flights, such as her long letter to Mrs. James. Here she loses the sprightliness and daintiness which are the characteristics of her style at its best, becomes laboured and artificial and generally ineffective. Probably she never would have become a great writer in the full acceptation of the term. Her gifts were in a comparatively narrow compass, and when she stepped outside her natural boundaries she lost her bearings. But her letters as a whole will live as the reflections of a vivid mind, delightful in their play of a delicate fancy and their sure use of a capacity for satire which is the more effective as it is never malicious.

And their personal qualities do not alone constitute the title of her letters to enduring fame. In her descriptions of life and her narration of facts she supplies a record which is of high historical value. With her graphic pages before us we obtain a truer conception than is to be gained from more serious literature of an India in violent transition, and of an Anglo-Indian society which was rapidly emerging from the unpretentious dullness and mercantilism of the factory period of British rule. For these gifts we have reason to be grateful to her. They make us a little blind to her faults and dispose us to be very kind to her virtues.

Resting in her little space of hallowed ground in the western city, Eliza conveys to us by her writings an impression of intellectual womanhood, wayward and impulsive, lacking, it may be, in moral fibre, but possessing to the full the finer attributes which in all ages have constituted the most potent element of female attractiveness. There is no need to indulge a lachrymal enthusiasm for her after the manner of Sterne, or to rhapsodize over her in the style of the Abbé Raynal. But we may at least preserve some kindly and generous thoughts for one who, even if the worst construction is to be put upon her actions, was probably more sinned against than sinning.

DESCENT *of* ELIZABETH DRAPER

- CHRISTOPHER SCLATER (4th in descent from Anthony Sclater) Vicar of Chingford (1681–1737) = 1708, ELIZABETH (1685–1743), d. of John May, of Worting, Hants
  - RICHARD SCLATER (1711–1754) = (1) 1738, MAGDALEN, d. of John Limbrey; (2) 1751, PENELOPE, d. of Philip Lutley
    - (by 1) THOS. LIMBREY SCLATER (1742–1809)
    - (by 1) ELIZABETH SCLATER (1744–1814)
    - (by 2) BARTHOLOMEW LUTLEY SCLATER (1753–1804)
      - WILLIAM LUTLEY SCLATER (1789–1885)
        - GEORGE SCLATER-BOOTH, 1st Lord Basing (1826–1894)
          - GEORGE LIMBREY 2nd Lord Basing (born 1860)
        - PHILIP LUTLEY SCLATER (1829–1913)
          - WILLIAM LUTLEY SCLATER (born 1863)
    - (by 2) PENELOPE LUTLEY SCLATER (1752–1843)
  - WILLIAM SCLATER, D.D., of Bow Church (1709–1773)
  - CHRISTOPHER SCLATER (1713)
  - JOSEPH SCLATER (1715–1769)
  - MAY SCLATER (1719–1746?) = JUDITH, d. of Chas. Whitehill
    - ELIZABETH (1744–1778) = DANIEL DRAPER (1726–1805)
      - Son (1759–1769)
      - ELIZABETH (1761–) = 1785, THOS. NEVILL
        - Son
        - 3 Daughters
    - MARY (1745–1762) = RAWSON HART BODDAM (1734–1812)
      - CHAS. BODDAM (1762–1811) = CHARLOTTE, d. of Col. Barrington
        - GEORGE RAWSON BODDAM
        - 2 Daughters (one Mrs. LISLE HALL, died about 1869)
    - LOUISA = COL. PEMBLE
  - ELIZABETH (1714–1769) = Rev. THOS. PICKERING, of St. Sepulchre's, London

Index

N